I0519349

Women OF THE HEBREW Bible

Their Stories

Women OF THE HEBREW Bible

Their Stories

DANIEL H. RONIS
and
DONNA SOMERVILLE

BIG MOOSE
PUBLISHING

©2023 Daniel H. Ronis and Donna Somerville. All rights reserved.
Cover Design and Interior Design Credit: Fay Thompson of Big Moose
Publishing
Cover Art Credit: K.L. Pavier
Published by: Big Moose Publishing
PO Box 127 Site 601 RR#6 Saskatoon, SK CANADA S7K 3J9
www.bigmoosepublishing.com

All rights reserved. No part of this book may be used or reproduced by any
means, graphic, electronic, or mechanical, including photocopying, recording,
taping or by any information storage retrieval system without the written
permission of the publisher except in the case of brief quotations embodied
in critical articles and reviews.

Because of the dynamic nature of the Internet, any web addresses or links
contained in this book may have changed since publication and may no longer
be valid. The views expressed in this work are solely those of the author and
do not necessarily reflect the views of the publisher, and the publisher hereby
disclaims any responsibility for them.

ISBN: 978-1-989840-65-8 (sc)
ISBN: 978-1-989840-66-5 (e)
Big Moose Publishing 01/24

DEDICATION

*For the women of the Hebrew Bible
and their enduring faith*

CONTENTS

PREFACE

This is a channelled book, conceived in the best traditions of Edgar Cayce, Jane Roberts, and others who have contributed greatly to our understandings by accessing non-conventional sources of information. The impetus for this book came a few years ago when I (Dan) started to pull together small bits of channelled information concerning the ancient Hebrews from various books. Those included The Seth Material (J. Roberts), The Only Planet of Choice (P.V. Schlemmer), Revelations for a New Millennium (A. Ramer) and others. The information I compiled was fascinating and significantly differed from the Biblical text, but was incomplete and fragmentary. There was no full story of any of the persons or events of the Hebrew Bible.

This led me to contact Donna Somerville, who had previously given me several personal readings, to see if she could access information concerning ancient Biblical times. The result was beyond all expectations. We put together an incredible book about the main characters and events of the Hebrew Bible, from Adam and Eve to Moses, which will be published at a later date.

Then, we created this book, specifically about women of the Hebrew Bible and their stories. This book began with a simple question: Why are the Matriarchs (Sarah, Rebekah, and Rachel) given a prominent place in the Bible and even in traditional prayers, yet very little is said about them? Is there a bigger, fuller story? Is there more to their story than giving their handmaidens to their husbands to produce children, then scheming to have their favourite son get the father's blessing, or stealing idols? The answer is a resounding yes. There is so much more to their stories and lives.

However, the overarching question I wanted to have answered was, "Why were women written about so badly, so negatively in the Hebrew Bible, even heroic women like Esther?" There is also some diminishing of the women's stature, even as they are praised. I found the answers; and these women shine brightly for their leadership, faith, teachings, and love of learning. These answers also reveal why I deliberately left Leah out of the above list of Matriarchs.

This is a Q&A channelled book which means that the structure is a series of questions asked by me (Dan Ronis) during the sessions that are immediately answered by Donna Sommerville while in conscious trance. Instead of labelling each paragraph as Q or A, they are labeled as DR and DS to designate who is speaking. A list of questions was prepared in advance for each biblical woman to be investigated, but were not given to Donna beforehand. The questions were read one at a time by me (Dan) during the session and additional questions arose as each answer was given by Donna. In this way, all answers were spontaneous and not even the topic to be addressed was known in advance by Donna.

The notations used throughout the book, such as "**#1 Recording 7:44** *The Nature of Eve's Soul*" refer to each sequential recorded session. #1 denotes the first session, the time the entry began, here at minute 7:44, and a topic reference. These notations are simply for us to track each entry and ensure accuracy. All entries were recorded for this book except where noted as "from Book 1".

Some of the chapters have a discussion section which took place after the channeled section. This was a free-form discussion between me and Donna after the channelled session had ended. We included parts that added to the information about the biblical person in question and often brought out more details that Donna was aware of, but had not spoken of in trance.

Enjoy the stories.

A NOTE FROM DAN

I n the Beginning, with the creation of the first fully conscious, sentient humans, there was equality between male and female, Adam and Eve. They were different in many ways, yet complemented each other and learned from each other in this new life on Earth. After Eden, there was a lessening of equality, but during the time of the Matriarchs, there was still near-equality between leaders of the tribe, Abraham and Sarah. What happened after that in terms of power imbalance between the sexes is unfortunate, and perhaps started from the time of Dinah and continued afterwards.

There are two forces at work here: one is the actual change in power imbalance that started long ago and the other is the written story of power imbalance. Although both have led to millennia of wrongness, the latter has been used to justify the continuation of this imbalance up to the present day and, thus, structures and maintains this societal issue.

Bible stories such as Eve being blamed for the forbidden fruit, the rape of Dinah, or Miriam challenging Moses' marriage with their subsequent consequences, are difficult to explain or justify. Fortunately, our channelled answers differ significantly from these Bible stories. In each case, there were actual events involving these women, but the stories were written differently from what likely happened. It appears that the Bible stories were written to create a moral lesson regarding disobedience as well as to unfairly place blame on women. The stories we present are more believable, rational, acceptable and, in my opinion, likely closer to the truth. In some cases, such as with Eve and Dinah, there was no relation of the biblical story to the story we found, that is no apple, no rape. In other cases, such as the incident involving Rachel and the idols, there was a removal of idols, but for different reasons than given.

The channeled stories in this book are biographical, depicting various women, their thoughts, feelings, leadership, teachings and roles in the Hebrew tribes. Eve and the Matriarchs were leaders and teachers, especially of the women, and brave, supportive, and strong. They were respected by their husbands and the tribe and were not treated as second class citizens. The channelled answers did not support the stories of men taking more than one wife nor the stories of the Patriarchs having children with their wives' handmaidens. Whoever wrote these stories that way is unknown, but their intention is seemingly dishonest.

Since many of the stories in the Hebrew Bible are difficult to accept at face value, there have been countless attempts to explain, justify, and understand these difficult biblical passages. The stories we have provided via this channelling are far more believable, rational, and require less mental contortions to accept. The stories are far more detailed and the personalities of the women clearly emerge as the questions posed are answered. Our hope by providing these stories is to begin to reverse the damage caused to societies and to male-female relationships by establishing stories that present these admirable women in a far better light. If we can help to re-establish balance in society and remove the biblical stories as a source to justify inferior roles for females, it would be a wonderful accomplishment.

Dan Ronis

A NOTE FROM DONNA

As we explored the story of Eve, in essence, the beginning of a new kind woman on Earth, new ideas and possibilities came to light. These are all contained within this book and offered for you to consider. There is, however, some brief explanations required of the use of language and what it refers to.

This book is not the first channelling we did to explore the "story" of mankind on the Earth. In the first channelling, an observing council came through that needed to be called "The Counsel". The Counsel, overall, did not play a large part in the channeling of this book, except in Section One, the story of EVE. Here The Counsel plays a large role.

You will notice places where the pronoun "we" is used, and it is used to express someone observing the situation or development of Eve and the women of the times. This "we" is The Counsel originally encountered in our previous channelings.

You can hear The Counsel in word expressions such as "it was fascinating to watch" and that is because The Counsel was doing simply that, "watching". They did not interfere, but rather watched the development on the Earth at that time, as if it was an experiment.

The same is true in Chapter Two. In Eden, when The Counsel is describing how Eve adapted to being in a human body, the viewpoint of this description is that of The Counsel.

In Section Two Matriarchs, "we" referred to a gathering of Matriarchal presence. But in the chapter on Eve, it is a totally different use of the pronoun "we" and now refers to "The Counsel".

And further in Chapter Two when the statement is made "This be the struggles that we can speak to you of.", this is to acknowledge that it is The Counsel recalling their observations of how Eve and those around her evolved at that time.

Donna Somerville

Section One

EVE

So the Lord cast a deep sleep upon the man; and, while he slept, He took one of his ribs and closed up the flesh at that spot. And the Lord fashioned the rib that he had taken from the man into a woman; and he brought her to the man. (Genesis 2:21-22)

Chapter One

BEFORE EDEN

#2 Recording 20:55 (from Book 1) *Eve Created from Adam's Rib*

DR: What part of Adam was used to create Eve and was it in that order, first male, then female?

DS: The first body created was androgynous. In creating the second, part of the distinct difference was the creation of the male to female. And energetically from Creation, the god and goddess; the male energy, the female energy; the thinking energy, the feeling energy. And so the difference in gender was a way of marking the difference in energy, and then also to ensure that procreation could occur. There was a question whether the procreation would occur, and so they were created so that it was possible, but whether it would happen was not clear. **The myth of the rib of Adam feels to be more because the cells of the marrow in the bone were part of the basic recipe of the second body.** But the DNA was altered, and the energy brought into the body was altered. Again, I feel this science counsel, in an experiment on the Earth and creation energies, using the science counsel to evolve so much more than another life form. As if there was a science experiment on the planet Earth by a species. But also, creation forces using inspired ideas to the science forces to experiment so much further than they realized. Understood?

DR: Yes.

#2 Recording 24:24 (from Book 1) Creation of Male –Female Differences

DR: So the human body that was created from the life force was at first androgynous and then basically split in two, into male and female? It was almost a split, rather than one created from the other?

DS: One was created and it was androgynous, and then there was the inspiration to create a second, from part of the first body *(feels like bone marrow was used)* with alterations. And that is when the concept of procreation, male-female, though I am not sure those were the words used, but that was when that concept was born. So, one was not really made from the other, but the seed of the second body came from the marrow, and then it was created separately. It felt important to the experiment and **very** important to CREATION, that there was a distinct difference being in this pair. Even more so than other pairs that had been created. It was almost like a graduation, on a science level, of creation – how different the pairs could be. It's like the humans were the graduation of creation for that science council and for CREATION itself, and experimentation with energy. What we would call male-female energy. But the energy was ordered in such a way that the science council could not anticipate where this would go. Because CREATION itself did not want to plan where this would go. It was a sense of a freedom to evolve. And so the energies wanted to be similar, but also distinctly different.

Two halves of the same whole, but also distinctly different... harmonious, but different. And it feels like from the science council perspective, this was the graduation of creation, as if they created animals or insects or other lower level creations and then the human creation was the graduation of it. Understood?

DR: Yes.

[Note: Bone marrow cells are stem cells and retain the ability to differentiate into any kind of cell.]

#1 Recording 7:44 The Nature of Eve's Soul

DR: We want to explore the women in the Bible and their role. In a previous channelling we received, it was stated about Eve that: "*it was a raw soul essence, raw potential, and aided and affected the dance between the Adam and Eve*".* (The Counsel)

Can you please explain more about the nature of the soul of Eve?

DS: This soul was new to incarnation, had never incarnated on a planet such as Earth. There had been previous incarnations, but brief and in different dimensions of space. She did not hold many memories. There was an innocence in her, a youthful vibrancy, and that was important. There needed to be a **child-like trust**. This is the word that is strongest.

We are suggesting that the essence of Eve had a trust within it, and also a deep knowing. Through that innocent trusting that would be called child-like in your language, there was an awareness of things, of people and places; an understanding of people, of places, and that allowed her to be like a sponge. She could hear, see, feel so much, and took so much of it in.

Had such a being been brought to your planet now, she would be overwhelmed and perhaps lose her mind. But the place where she was created was quiet, reserved, clear, and so it was with this beautiful perfection that she entered the being-ness of Eve.

It did initially create certain problems in her dance with the Adam, because they were quite different. But as they came into the being-ness of the human, they each had something to teach the other. The experiential memories of Adam could teach Eve things that she had never experienced. And the open trust of Eve could bring to Adam ideas, patience, kindnesses that he had not experienced in his memory. And so there was this beautiful symbiotic dance, and it enhanced the learning of the two of them.

We are also going to suggest that it was easier for Eve to accept the perfections of Eden than for Adam, because she did not have the expectation of imperfection. We do not say that she even understood perfect or imperfect. It is just that she could accept what Eden offered. She could accept what Eden was, in a way that Adam sometimes struggled with. She was more open to it, more able to receive it and accept it.

This also translated into the dance with Adam. We suggest that Eve was more open and able to accept Adam, who he was, how he was. Where Adam still had some memories that did create within him small judgments. And so there were times where Eve could accept more of Adam than Adam could accept of Eve. It was magnificent to see this trusting soul, open to experience what the life could be like with Adam, with Eden.

Everything she experienced she was with it. Nothing happened to her; she was with it. She was with nature and with the animals and with the Adam, and with what Eden offered to her. So there was a clarity and a lack of unconscious memory. We will not say that this lasted the whole of her lifetime, because it did not. And as we watched her evolve, we could see memory forming and that in and of itself was a fascinating experience, to watch her unconscious develop and fill with memories. But hers did not fill so quickly because there were very few things she could not accept. As she aged, as others joined in the family, in the birthing of children, there were more things she struggled with accepting. For those first decades her acceptance was almost unconditional. It was fascinating to watch.

#1 Recording 13:29 *Eve's Decision to Incarnate*

DR: Was it her decision to accept this incarnation? Was she asked to do it? Did she volunteer?

DS: There was great interest caught by many in the universe as the Earth entered this next stage of development. And as we have already spoken, there is a uniqueness to your planet. There were many souls interested in incarnating in such a place, experiencing such a development as Evolution. And so there were souls who came, who had not yet experienced Evolution elsewhere, so they too had no memory of Evolution.

To answer your question specifically, Eve's soul was willing, volunteering to be part of an incarnation in a place that had Evolution. She had never experienced Evolution before and there was a curiosity in her soul, right from the beginning. There was an intent within her soul to incarnate here several times so that the Evolution could be experienced over a period of time. The soul volunteered for more than one incarnation, from the very beginning.

Again, there is that beautiful innocent trust within the essence of Eve that embraced the experience completely, without trepidation, without caution, without hesitation. And so in answer to your question, she was a volunteer and did incarnate subsequent lifetimes after the lifetime of Eve.

#1 Recording 15:26 Eve's Subsequent Incarnations

DR: Can you talk about subsequent incarnations? Was she a person of note when she was in that tribe with the Hebrews? What was the nature of her incarnations?

DS: She stayed with the humans; she did not incarnate to humanoid (the primitive creatures already on Earth). Her first lifetime was a long one. It was five generations from her first child; five generations that she incarnated, again as a female. Again, she brought in some memories from the Eden and was able to hold those tribal memories from the Eden. As a child she knew things that amazed her parents about their own history.

Her incarnations were female, and each incarnation was quite long. We would say that Eve's first incarnation was three generations long, into the fourth. She returned to incarnation again. She went through her process to prepare to return and returned to incarnated form in what would have been the fifth generation.

That lifetime she lived would be the equivalent of three generations now. And again, she took a generation to debrief (*for lack of a better word*) and then incarnated again, twelve generations from Eve.

It becomes harder to count and to explain, as we get further away from the first lifetime as Eve.

She had five lifetimes on the Earth, the first of which was Eve. They were almost consecutive with decades, maybe even a hundred years between them. Always female. She wanted to track one lifetime after another. She wanted to experience consecutive lifetimes with her memories. And we would say of the five lifetimes, the first three she came in with her memories. And so, she was important to the tribe she was born into, for she could confirm memories, confirm information, confirm history.

The last two incarnations, the memories were much degraded and one of those final two lifetimes she lived a difficult life, a life direct to those from Eden, but in a difficult place, in a different place. No longer sharing memories, no longer clear of memories, no longer in that joyous happiness that she had in the other lifetimes. But that was deliberate as well. The soul wanted to take the experiences of the previous lifetimes into two final lifetimes that were very different. She was in the line of Eve, meaning she followed that same soul family through all of the lifetimes. We also want to say that in terms of what your words would describe as "important", she was becoming less and less important in those lifetimes.

In the first three lifetimes she held an importance. She was important in the teachings of the origins of Eden, maintaining the shared beliefs, and the shared memories. But as the memories degraded, she also wanted to experience the lifetimes that were degraded and so the last two lifetimes were not the joyous, connected awareness that she had experienced in the first three. Her soul grew beautifully, and deliberately chose these lifetimes. There was no happenstance. There was no accident here.

In the fifth lifetime, she even experienced disease, discomfort, lack, hurt. But we will not say she never experienced hurt before, just not this way. In that fifth lifetime, she chose a place where hurt would be inflicted purposely, on purpose. She had not experienced that in the other four lifetimes.

The soul wanted to see what the Evolution was offering and wanted to evolve with the evolution of the place, of the beings, of the humans as they moved further and further from the Eden moment.

#1 Recording 20:45 *Eve's Incarnation – Mother of Moses*

DR: When she was in the line of Eve, was she married to, or the daughter of, any person noted in the Hebrew Bible in that lineage from Adam?

DS: The one place that we feel certain is that she was the mother of Moses. And that is why she could bring to him such teachings with such determination and why she commanded such respect.

The others we do not see clearly. I am trying to follow the

timelines in my vision, but they are not clear. No. The others are not clear.

The only one I can speak with certainty is that she was the mother of Moses.

Chapter Two

IN EDEN

#1 Recording 22:19 *Eve's Struggles in Her First Lifetime*

DR: What struggles did she have with adapting to Earth and being in a body on Earth?

DS: The fragility of a body; the cutting of a finger, the bruise of an arm. She had not been in a body this way before, but interestingly she would have us correct your language. It was not a struggle. It was an adventure. It was a discovery,. *That is the word*; it was a discovery.

But the fragility of the body... how easily the body could be damaged, that was interesting. Of course, in the first times in Eden any damage was repaired immediately, and so there was no suffering nor hurt. And that was something that the soul wanted to study, *if that is the right word*, because this one had not experienced hurt or damage to herself in other lifetimes. She had not incarnated in a dimension quite so dense that could allow for damaging.

As she aged, in the latter decades of her life, the struggle she would answer you with is the struggle of accepting others' choices... the dynamic of different choices among the children, the grandchildren, the tribe. When all choices were for the good of all it was an interesting dance. But, when the choices started to become more selfish in nature, she struggled terribly with that acceptance, and there were times she did try to inflict her will, "stand in her power" are the words you would use, to demand a different or better, what she would call, a better behavior. But they fell on deaf ears, because when that willfulness was developing in a selfish way, it was quite deaf. She did still command respect in the family line and was listened to perhaps seventy-five percent of the time. So, to use your words, "her struggle" was with that twenty-five percent of the time where she was ignored, disregarded. And then dealing with the emotional ramifications of that, but again, that was not until outside of the Eden times.

Within Eden everything was cushioned, everything was felt, everything happened, but it was brief and it was healed quickly. It was completed quickly. There was no suffering in Eden. And so, when the suffering began, the selfishness began. Then the emotions within herself and reactions to the suffering in the heart began; this was enlightening. At first fascinating, and then just hurtful. She struggled with the disregard. She struggled with the selfishness.

There is an aspect to this soul essence that has held, still holds, its childish innocent expectations, hopeful wonder. Her soul has managed to hold that through all of the incarnations upon the Earth in the evolutions, and she did struggle the most with that in those early decades after Eden. To see and understand and not know what to do to cope, because that innocent trust gave her this understanding, this awareness of what was going on. But what to do about it? This was the confusion. And when will didn't work, what to do about it then? And then it became complicated by her emotional reactions, her emotional responses, to feel personally hurt.

The very first time was an overwhelming experience, and took her days to recover from it, to feel an emotional woundedness. This was something never encountered before in any other lifetime. And yet there was also, at a soul level, an excitement, because this is why the soul came to the planet, to watch that evolution, that another might call degradation, of the perfection of Eden into what it would become.

There was also a learning from those first emotional hurts that took days to recover from. This created a closeness with other females, a sharing with other females, because of the nurturance in the females. Among themselves they were trying to find a way to heal each other, but it wasn't a wound that could be wrapped, or a poultice applied. It was an inner wound, and the exploration of what that felt like, what that meant, led to the beginnings of that sisterhood that developed among the females after Eden. It led to an understanding in the females of the growth of emotions and their reactions in choice. It led to sharing among the females that the males knew very little about.

The females could understand things of the emotions that the males could not. We would say to you now, that it was tied, very tied, to the procreation. But it was not understood that it was tied to procreation at that time. There was an open awareness left in the mothers of the children so that the children could be kept safe, so that the mothers could hear, know their children always, so they could care for them as they needed, knowing in advance what they needed. That openness allowed them to be more susceptible to the emotional hurt, to the hurt of selfishness. But it also allowed them, when they came together, to be able to find ways to nurture that emotional hurt, to heal that emotional hurt. It gave them an understanding of it. Eve tried to share this with Adam, but it was not understandable to him. He was open in a way that would not be recognizable to men of your era, but there was not the same openness that Eve had.

There was more retaliating than healing within Adam. And so he wanted to understand what Eve explained, but he wanted to retaliate for it. Whereas Eve wanted it to be healed, to be understood, to be patiently loved. And so her experience with emotional hurt and the emotional selfishness was very different in the female line than in the male line.

We have spoken already about the violence and the blinded fury. *(This refers to earlier channeled information not contained in this book.)*

Females experienced this very differently. They experienced this as harmed inside, of the wound that they shared with the sisters and looked to understand, forgive, though they would not use the word forgive. Look to understand, become aware of and patient with, and try and soothe.

It was the beginning of something called "soothing of the soul". And the women would look to soothe the souls of their men, the souls of their sons, in a way that they did not have to soothe the souls of their daughters, or the souls of their sisters; but did need to soothe the souls of their fathers, their brothers, their husbands, their partners, their sons. And it started this dynamic growth in understanding of how the female related to this willful developing choice. And so she (Eve) struggled with this and yet, it was paramount in her learning, in her experience of the lifetime, and she pursued this in other lifetimes.

It is why in the lifetime as the mother of Moses, there were complications in her lifetime. She married an Egyptian. She raised her son Hebrew. She wanted to be forthright and honest. She dealt with her shame. She spoke the truth. She hid nothing, except with her son. She hid things from her son until her son was ready to know. She did not hide herself, but she did not put her beliefs on display. She was the representative of truth and that integrity, that radiant strength, allowed her to be who she was, as she was. And so she purposely walked in that lifetime, in what would be considered from the outside looking in, with more difficulty, more complication. These would be the struggles that we can speak to you of.

#1 Recording 32:53 Eve's Helpers

DR: When in Eden, did Eve have helpers? Were there humanoids? Did she have help?

{Note: When Adam and Eve were created, there were already primitive humans, humanoids or hominids, already on the earth. Adam and Eve were created with a higher level of consciousness to assist in the development of the earth. (from Book 1)}

DS: *Returning to the time of Eden, show me now please.*

At first there was no need for help, for they harvested and had what they needed when they needed it. And there was a long time that it was only the two. The need for help did not arise until outside of Eden. There is a sense of Eden being heaven-like, the word you would use to define it now in your world. Afterwards, there was a sharing. It wasn't so much that there was an employee or slave, or a maid; there was a sharing. For nearly three generations people came together to do something together, so there wasn't a sense of a single having to do for all. There was a sense of Eve having to do for all, through that first birth generation. But even then, there was not a lot of demand upon her. It was not a lot of people to feed, or people to care for. It wasn't until the first generation was grown to young adults that then the sharing began and the help she needed was there.

And again, that memory had an impact in the lifetime with Moses because she treated her servants, of which she had plenty, very differently than others around her, because in those Eden memories, it was not servitude, it was sharing. And so those helped others who needed help.

#1 Recording 35:13 *Food Sources in Eden*

DR: When in Eden, did Eve utilize the plants and animals? What kind of food was provided? Clothing?

DS: In the early stages, the food and clothing came from her beginnings, The Counsel. And things lasted a long time. They were in this timeless place. There was no changing of clothes; there was not a need for it, or a desire for it. There was relationship with the plants and animals. There was abundance.

There was a sense of what was needed was there when needed. There wasn't a sense within her to question it; it simply arrived. It was like they were thinking about what they would want to eat and there they would find it quite effortlessly. We do not mean that if they thought of eggs, there was a basket of eggs on a table. They would find the bird or the hen that would give up the eggs. The eggs would be present for them. They still had to collect them and make an effort, but they did not have to hunt far for what they needed. It does not feel like they killed and ate meat. It feels like they took the offerings of animals and the offerings of plants. Perhaps in your language we would say they were more vegetarian, and the meat would only be eaten when an animal died. There was no fear of disease so we cannot tell you how the animal died. We see two or three instances where an animal dies and meat is enjoyed but it is not common. It might be once a year.

After Eden, things changed. They had never known hunger in Eden. They had never known want in Eden. After Eden that changed. They did experience starvation, only the once. And then Adam organized the sons to ensure that did not happen again. And we want to say it never did.

There was more effort required, and they began eating meat when the climates changed and the colds came, as if the body could not generate enough warmth with only the plants. They became meat eaters in the cold. They were meat eaters in the cold and vegetable eaters in the warm. It was always adaptive; it was always a decision adaptive to the situation.

The generation around Adam and Eve only starved once, and from then on Adam ensured it would not happen. The tribes did not starve often. It was almost as if it was part of the teachings, part of the learnings. More the men than the females, but everyone knew what starvation was and how to ensure it did not occur again.

#1 Recording 38:52 Myth of the Forbidden Fruit

DR: Will you explain the myth of Eve eating the forbidden fruit and giving some to Adam, that is in the Bible?

DS: This is connected to the starvation, the meat eating, and the harvesting of animals. We would say to you that what is called in your myth, the apple, is meat. The evil of it was the killing of the animal, making the needs of men's hunger more important than the animal's presence. That was first seen as evil, *that's not the right word*, but it was shocking. *That's the word!* It was **shocking.** When there was starvation, Adam was desperate and so he killed a live animal, a live healthy animal, roasted the meat, ate some of it raw. But that seemed to create sickness, so then it was cooked. And it feels to us that it was Adam's doing, not Eve's. The children were sick. They were starving, and Eve was with child and starving. Adam flew into a rage of fear. It was in the cold and there were no plants to harvest; the ice, there was no fish to fish. So Adam, in a fury, killed a live, healthy animal. And what later became your Myth of Evil, the Knowledge of Good and Evil, was the knowledge of making man's needs more important than anything else.

The killing, the selfish need answered, but his family survived. There was shame in him for having killed such a healthy animal. They had not deliberately killed a healthy animal so viciously before. They had taken the weak ones from the herd. They had taken the young ones, deformed, from the herd. They had eaten meat, but this was decisive, deliberate, and it was the state of the health of the animal. Also, because the animals had not been hunted, the animal did not know to run.

The animal was the victim of Adam and that was the grain, the seed, of what later became your Myth of Evil. It was a selfish act for selfish need. It feels to us that it occurred with Adam to ensure the survival of his family.

How did this become put upon the shoulders of Eve, please show me now?

There was such shame in Adam afterwards, the emotional hurt we spoke of. It was deep in him, and Eve could feel it and see it. We want to say being with child she was even more sensitively aware to his shame and his hurt and we want to say to you that we witnessed Eve take the blame; tell to Adam that she was the one that called him to do it so that the children would survive, so that the unborn child would survive. She offered to him that when others asked, he could tell them it was for her; it was her that needed, her that asked, her that demanded.

Adam never used the word demand, but the story did begin that it was Eve's idea to kill a healthy animal, to victimize such an animal. And it came to be put upon the shoulders of Eve by Eve's own agreement. It was her effort to take some of Adam's shame away. She was able to convince him that it was her and her children that needed it and so it was her to blame. In his hurtfulness, he could accept that. But when we looked inside him there was still a grain that he always knew the truth, but it was not spoken.

I cannot see how the tree or the apple or the snake come into being.

Though when we explore the snake, it is lies, cheating, murderous intent of taking the animal's life. But I cannot see how this became a snake.

DR: This happened after leaving Eden?

DS: Yes, because there was no possibility of starvation in Eden. It was after Eden.

#1 Recording 45:21 Eve Communicating with Adam

DR: How did Eve and Adam communicate? What kind of language or communication did they have? Were they both new to being human?

DS: In Eden, in the first stage of Eden, it was telepathy. Eyes knowing, hearing, open-mindedness. But that did not last long, and it was interesting to watch that telepathy degrade. We (The Counsel) did not understand until much later how that occurred. We allowed it to occur; we would not interfere. And we did not understand how it occurred. And as our beliefs have always shown, time would show us how it occurred. And it did. Later, we understood that it was in fact Evolution that degraded the telepathy. But we did not know it at the time. We simply watched the telepathy degrade. And as the telepathy degraded, they moved to hand signals and then sounds, and then from the sounds your languages developed.

But that took generations, two, three generations before you would call it a language. But initially it was telepathy. There was a knowing between them, a shared understanding between them. It was easier for Eve than Adam. But it was Eve's openness and her ease with the open-mindedness that encouraged Adam to be of the same. And again, because this was a new experience of incarnation, there was an eagerness in each of them to experience all that was possible. As so there was not a lot of caution. We would say there was no caution to the experiment of it. It wasn't until the second generation that there was more close-mindedness. Even in Eden, there was the beginnings of close-mindedness. But it was the second generation where the close-mindedness really necessitated language.

#1 Recording 47:45 Eve Interacting with Humanoids

DR: The woman companions you mentioned with Eve, especially after Eden, were these humanoids?

DS: We want to say no.

Creator of All That Is show me the images, show me the time line, now please.

After Eden there was a sense of keeping to themselves. They were aware of the humanoids, but they were also aware of how different they were to the humanoids. Though the humanoids, as Eve could perceive them, did have shared memories, they were not as open-minded as the line of Adam and Eve.

It was the children, the offspring assisting the parents. The parents assist the offspring. It was quite a few generations; we would say four generations. It is hard to see because of that timelessness. I want to say that four generations after the fall of Eden before humanoid interaction occurred. We will not say they did not ever interact, but they did not do so deliberately. They were aware of each other. They had learned through sign language to communicate with each other. There was an open-mindedness that was simpler in the humanoids, but still available to Adam and Eve and so there was communication, but it was only if they happened upon each other. For the most part they kept away.

The stronger the differences between Adam and Eve and the humanoids, the further they stayed away, and the longer they stayed away. It wasn't until the differences were a little less, until the humanoids had more similarities to the methods, to the tools, to the ways of being.

#1 Recording 50:08 Eve with the Three Created Females

DR: In an earlier channeling, it was mentioned that there were three other pairs, besides Adam and Eve, created. Did Eve interact with the other three females?

DS: In the early stages of Eden, yes. They had teachings to share with each other. They had experiences one would have that the other did not. So, there was story telling between them, sharing between them. They helped each other grow, with understanding, enlightenment, realization of being alive.

The other females were also fairly new souls but not as new as Eve, and so they had a few more memories. Not as many memories as the males, but some memories. There was experimentation with the females, learning with the females. It was particularly around hunger and the answer to hunger, physical hunger.

There was not yet a sisterhood in the early stage of Eden. The sisterhood did not come until after Eden. But there was the beginning of a camaraderie, an awareness of the likes, of the ways they were similar. And there was a deep awareness of the differences. It was in the differences that they taught each other, shared with each other.

They did live separately; they did not live as one, under one roof. It was important to The Counsel that the differences be nurtured and allowed to grow and develop in the humans they were becoming. And so The Counsel did not want them all to be the same, and so as much as the females would share their differences, they did not change themselves for each other; and so they do not live as one. There was too much danger of being changed.

We (The Counsel) wanted differences between the pairs. We wanted the pairs to know of the differences, to respect the differences, but not expect the differences to align or change in any way.

It feels like there were more differences in the females than the males. But still there were distinct differences between the pairs and that came from their memories; it came from what each brought in.

As we have said, Eve brought in this innocent trust, this eager enthusiasm. It was not the same in the other females. This was unique to Eve.

I cannot see the other females well enough to read. Creator of All That Is, are we allowed to understand, perhaps the characteristics of another of the females of this early time in Eden? Show me now please.

Another came in strong, determined, brave. Very brave. Curious. Brave and curious. They fed each other. Eve's curiosity was like a child, a wonder. But this one had a bravery, an experimental curiosity. Stronger, more determined. And so they learned from each other's differences and differences in character, but did not adapt from one to another. They held their uniqueness as we had intended. We (The Counsel) do not know why. We intended it to be so. We did not interfere to make it so. But they did hold their uniqueness. We believe it's because we did not have them there as one family, under one roof. They lived in different parts, different sections, and were left to themselves for the most part.

Chapter Three

AFTER EDEN

#1 Recording 54:57 *Pairs Leaving Eden*

(Note: The reasons for leaving Eden are explained in detail in Book 1 and had nothing to do with expulsion by an angry God.)

DR: Did the pairs leave Eden together or separately? Did they interact after leaving Eden?

DS: The leaving of Eden feels traumatic. It feels fearful. It doesn't feel like there was a deliberate choice to go in different directions. They did not leave at the same time. They left at different times. They followed their own instincts of safety. And they followed their own inner guidance as to direction. We (The Counsel) do not know where the inner guidance came from. It did not come from what we implanted. But there did seem to be an inner awareness of safety. We watched them each have a different direction coming from their inner awareness of safety.

Adam and Eve were the last to leave for they were the most attached to the Eden place. And again, the different characteristics within them caused them to leave at different times.

The one that was brave and curious, that partner was also courageous and determined, and so they faced the danger bravely and left immediately. And so different characteristics within each affected the timing of when they left, how long they stayed, how long they were frightened, how long they were disoriented, and how long they were determined to become effective. Though we can say to you from our witness (The Counsel), that Adam and Eve were the last to leave the Eden place and they did not go far. Others went further away than Adam and Eve did, for they (Adam and Eve) were more attached to the Eden place.

#1 Recording 57:06 *Eve's Children and Timelessness*

DR: The Bible says that Adam lived 930 years and 800 years after Seth the third child was born and then he begot sons and daughters. So, if Adam had more sons and daughters after Seth, were these all born of Eve?

DS: Yes, it feels to us as if Eve was alive for what would be called three generations in your world. But again, the generations were much longer in the timeless realm. But the answer to your question is yes, she was the only mate of Adam. She was the only mother of his children.

They were in a timeless place in the early stages of Eden. In middle Eden times, there was some time developing. Again, we (The Counsel) did not develop it. It occurred. Awareness occurred, but it was nothing compared to the time of your world now. It was only the children after Seth where time was involved, and years could be put to them. That is why we are suggesting your years are put to them around the Seth time, because previous to that, they were timeless. So once time established itself, Eve was in three generations of childbearing and time established itself middle to the end of the Eden times, just before its collapse.

#1 Recording 58:57 Number of Children of Eve

DR: Can you tell us how many children Eve had, and did they all survive?

DS: The early births all survived. The births outside of Eden, not all survived.

How many children?

Eve was most often pregnant with very little time between conceptions. And so was pregnant for decades, longer than that. I want to say almost continually with child.

Very hard to see the answer to this question. Creator of All That Is, show me what is possible and ready to be known. Show me now please. The Counsel feels reluctant to answer this question. They are not hiding the answer exactly, but they are reluctant here. It is as if they don't want this information known. When I try to look deeper, they do not want Eve to be perceived as not a human. But to answer this question will make her seem less human in some way. She was human, they are adamant about that. They are adamant that she was human.

Her birthing process was not as you know birthing process now. It was accelerated. We (The Counsel) did not interfere with it, but it changed of its own accord after Eden. And there was a sense of more children after Eden. But we did not interfere with this.

We watched survival happen and we did not know what it was. The word we only learned through watching other times in your world. We did not know survival, but Eve made babies for her line to survive. And we watched it without understanding what we were seeing. She was still human. She bore humans, but the process was accelerated and the number of children she had is impossible in your world now for one woman. And so, we do not wish to answer this question in detail for it will make her seem inhuman and she was everything human. She brought to humanity's beginnings a specialness and we do not want that tarnished. And so, there is not a refusal, but a true resistance to answering this question.

#1 Recording 1:04:02 Birthing in Eden and Afterwards

DR: Who helped with her births and were the births much easier than it is for females later on?

DS: The births were very easy. There was never complication in Eden. We (The Counsel) had seen to the body being easily adapted to birth and it was beautiful to watch the body do as it was designed to do. And then after Eden, the births were different. There were sometimes complications. We did not interfere and when there were complications, we could glean the reasons: not enough food, not the right food, the temperatures, the weather, the fear, the travel. We could always glean a reason, but we did not interfere. The births became more difficult.

In the early births, there was absolutely no resistance within Eve to giving birth. It was a joyous gift she bestowed upon the planet, to Adam, to herself. It was blissful, beautiful. After Eden, it changed. We did not interfere, but it changed. There was still an ease in it, but there was sometimes some resistance, sometimes some reaction to the pregnancies. The emotional growth was affecting the births.

We have not come to full understanding of the births and the evolution of the birthing in those first generations after Eden. We watched it change. It took three generations to be different, five generations to really change and we merely watched it. We have not yet comprehension of what occurred, even though we had our understandings of the evolution, we do not understand what evolved. But we can say to you, the births at first were very easy, very beautiful, and then over hundreds of years, <u>hundreds</u> of years, it changed.

#1 Recording 1:07:12 Eve's Death

DR: So why does the Bible not mention Eve's death? Did she die before or after Adam?

DS: She died before Adam.

Show me the time lines please. (long pause......)

Her death was not from disease.

There is so much resistance to this being seen. *Creator of All That Is, if it is ready to be seen, show me now.*

It feels as if there was an accident. Killed by a retaliating animal, attacking animal. And there was much healing ability in those days, but the women, they could not stop the bleeding. And she bled to death from the wounds. There was blame laid. Fighting amongst the men. *Who was responsible?*

It was the first time Adam experienced the fury that he saw in his son's eyes, in the eyes of Cain.

He (Adam) experienced the same fury. It was ugly, blaming, divisive and so was ordered not to be told. It was too shaming to allow those stories to be told. And those stories, as stories told by the storytellers, were never told.

There was a group of eight men who knew of the occurrence, six women, and the story was never told. There was always a mystery around how she died. But we can see clearly, a cat, retaliating against the hunters. The hunters lost control of the cat. It reached the camp, took two children and Eve. There was no carnage or eating by the animal, but there was destruction with biting and claws. Those that died, bled to death.

There was fury in Adam. Fighting among the men, the hunters. Despair among the women. It was a great loss and one that was not understood. It broke something as if they believed that Eve was impervious to death, impervious to injury. She had never really been injured before. And so, the story was never told. Any story that would be told of Eve would be made up, because the accident was never spoken of. It was always a mystery.

It sent Adam into a very dark place, a fury. He destroyed many animals after that, in fury. And it took him months to come out of it. He had lost his sense, as if Eve was his sense, his conscience, and he had lost it. It took him years to recover his own sense, to find his own conscience, to replace her in his own self, and that too was never spoken of.

#1 *Recording 1:12:21 Eve Setting Pattern for Female Behaviour*

DR: So did Eve set the behaviour patterns for future females, wives, and mothers?

DS: Yes, and her death made them even more set-in stone. For there was a perfection in her that was viewed by others. She wasn't perfect, but if she was viewed as perfect and if she was not impervious to injury then the perfection became even more important. She had been an authority, a respected authority, gifted in awareness, gifted in understanding, patience and kindness. And all of those qualities became larger than life, after her passing. And from the mystery of her death those qualities became more important, almost required among the females. The six that nursed her and were present at her death, insured that what mattered to Eve would matter to the coming generations of females. They insured that what Eve believed would be set-in stone for females. And so, it is interesting that to answer your question we say, **"she did not make it the teaching of the females, but in her passing it became the teaching of the females"**.

Eve never required of people. She demonstrated and hoped that they would follow, and most did, but she was never stern; it was not in her nature. She was kind, and with her kindness she could persuade, with a patience, she could persuade, and was seldom said no to. But after, that is when it became almost set-in stone, required of the females, and it was the six females who nurtured her to her death that encountered that.

#1 Recording 1:14:42 *The Counsel's Concluding Remarks*

DS: *Creator of All That Is, is there further that can be added to this or are we complete for this day?*

We wish to explain what we witnessed. With the death of Eve, there was a change in the tribe, the females particularly, the six we have already mentioned. There is a word that appeared later in your evolution called *saint*. And if it had been present at the death of Eve, she would have been sainted. She became bigger than life. But what was most interesting was how she affected the upbringing of the girls, the training of the wives, the training of the grandmothers. For she had been grandmother, mother, sister, cousin to so many, whether by blood or not. And it was as if from there, the definitions of what those words meant and the requirements of those roles came from such a simple event – the death of a human – that affected the females in that line for generations. And there is still a lingering effect in your females now, a depth of understanding, an ability to kindness, an ability and awareness.

And as we witnessed this death of this one human, it was a ripple effect for generations. And we watched the changes, and those changes birthed other changes. And now we know the word for that: evolution.

We want to say to you that the death of Eve and the results from it also evolved. Truly in your world EVERYTHING evolves: reactions, responses, events. Evolution interweaves with all of it.

We did not, as the Counsel, for one moment consider replacing Eve. The experiment was too far along for any interference. And we were pleased that we did not interfere, because when we witnessed the ripple effect of Eve's death through the females and through the males from Adam; we want to describe it scientifically as the female's ripple effect reached through the generations in a vertical way, reached inside them, changed them, developed them. But the males, it is like it reached them horizontally and it changed them as well, but it seemed to give birth to protection and ownership, blame, and the rights of man to keep the family safe. It created the need for man to be protective.

And it feels like with the females it created a... *I don't know what word to use...* a higher, vertical evolution. But with males it's like they went sideways; they didn't evolve the way the females did. They adapted; they coped; and they created adapting behaviors, more protective, more violent, more structured, more predatory. It was amazing to see that affect everyone so differently, particularly from males to females.

I do not feel like I have the words correct because the image I'm seeing is the females evolved in a vertical way. But the males evolved in a horizontal way. But those words do not do justice to what I'm seeing.

The males did not grow from this event. The males coped from this event. The males developed coping mechanisms to this event, whereas the female grew from it. *Therein are the best words for this and the image I have* is the females growing vertically and the males growing horizontally; staying the same and adapting, staying the same and coping, more ownership, ownership of their females, ownership of their family, ownership of their home clan, protective of their home clan, predatory to anything that would threaten that clan.

The effect from the female line moved beyond, deep into the tribes. The effect from the males didn't move as far. I want to say five generations, four generations. Later the men softened and did not follow the coping mechanisms that came from Adam's reactions and responses, because they didn't follow forward; it was horizontal. And so, we want to say it limited the growth of the males, but did not stop it. It just stalled it for a while, three, four generations.

Chapter Four

OTHER WOMEN OF EDEN

#2 Recording 1:57 *Children of Other Created Women*

DR: A quick follow up to last time we talked about Eve and Eden, the other three women who were created along with Eve, did the other women have children and were there matings between the children of each woman?

DS: *Moving into Eden, show me now please.*

We can see the three other females created and it feels as if two are full adult. The third one feels slightly younger, as if it was wanted that this one would grow into womanhood. Not a child, perhaps thirteen, to grow into womanhood, watching and experiencing the womanhood of the other two. So there would be more experience in the third one.

All three had mates and the youngest one's mate was as young as she was. There was an understanding that they would be mated, as they grew. As expected, the first two had children before the third. The first one had children in Eden time. But it feels as if the second and third, *unclear*, their children did not come until after the Eden time. After they had left Eden, *but I'm not certain of that*. There are children to all three and generations did continue from these original three.

DR: So, the children of the original pairs did inter-mate with each other?

DS: Yes, but we (The Counsel) ensured that the DNA structures were such that there was enough difference so that the daughter of the first, could mate with the son of the second and the daughter of the third could mate with the son of the second. So, the DNA structure was different enough; we ensured that.

DR: So, they didn't mate with brother and sister? They mated with children of the other Earth pairs?

DS: Yes, there was no mating within the same line.

#2 Recording 5:47 Incarnations of the Other Three Women

DR: So did the other three women, aside from Eve, also have more incarnations, and were any of them a person of note?

#2 Recording 6:10 *First Woman – Life and Incarnations*

DS: *Following the first one, show me now please.*

The first one, as with Eve, lived a long time in the Eden time in that timeless realm. Once she left Eden, she still lived longer than you would expect now. She was on the Earth a long time and so there was quite a bit of time before this one left the Earth.

Accessing her leaving point in showing me the soul journey, show me now.

This one was well and truly ready to leave the Earth when she passed. She had lived hundreds of years by that point. And she was well proud of what had been established in their region of the Earth. When she left, she felt as if she had accomplished her purpose. When she moved into soul journey, she did witness the evolution on the Earth and chose to return to the Earth, but not for a while as if she was waiting for certain points of change, certain points of evolution to occur. At this point, we (The Counsel) had nothing to do with her journey further. We allowed the soul to make its own choices. We had started a process and left the rest to the soul journey.

She witnessed growth on the Earth, until the time of Moses, and then returned to the incarnation at that time. At the soul level, she understood the changes that had occurred in what was seeded in Eden and did return with a purpose to strengthen beliefs and the origins of Eden. She had memories. She came in as a female but still had memories, which was a bit difficult for her to be taken with seriousness, but when others of the male elders could confirm her memories, they did take her with seriousness.

We cannot attach a name of importance to this one but can say that she was important in discussions. Feels to us as if she was married to one of the three that helped Moses create the original rules, and she did help her husband confirming details. It feels as if she was married to the youngest of the three that assisted Moses, and that youngster did not have memories. And so, it was an interesting experience for him to have a wife who did. It did make him valuable to the council of the tribe, as the rules were first created.

It is interesting to us that those that she gave birth to also held the memories for three generations. More often, the memories were more easily respected in her sons than her daughters, but all of her children held the memories. It was as if her purpose was to re-energize, re-strengthen, the memories that had been fading in some of the elders around Moses' time.

DR: Could she have been married to Joshua, who was younger than Moses and Moses' helper?

DS: *Creator of All That Is, show me Joshua.*

We would say yes that she was married to Joshua. Further questions of this one, before we explore the other two?

DR: No, that is good. Thank you.

#7 Recording 30:31 Joshua's wife

DR: Joshua's wife, Joshua the helper of Moses, what was her role?

DS: Quiet, soft spoken, a very strong maternal energy, a mother of all. She would be mothering to many, adults and children. Quiet, soft, loving, very agreeable. It feels like her attention was much more focused on youngsters and children, the children of the tribe. There's a teacher in her heart and a caregiver in her heart. Any concerns she would voice to her husband was so that the future of the children would be strong, would be protected, would be faithful. She did not care about power or rules; her care was all dedicated to the children. Her opinions always looked to the future of the tribe in the future for the children. She was a strong voice among the women because, for some reason, she had a wonderful wisdom about children, the teaching of them, the raising of them, and the teaching of the basic skills that children need. She had innovative ways of training the children, from potty training, to speaking, to walking. She was very good with the other women to help them with their own mothering and teaching skills. She was the quiet voice in the tribe that spoke through the children. She cared for the children; she taught the children; she raised the children. She helped to raise them. It feels to us as if her influence was completely through the children.

Understood?

DR: Yes.

#7 Recording 32:52 Joshua's wife

DR: Is there a name for her, Joshua's wife?

DS: The naming is very uncertain. It feels like her name at birth starts with an R. I don't think it's Ruth, but it feels like she was called something else – some form of Mama, but it wasn't

Mama. It was something that recognized her as the maternal energy that she was. I'm not sure, but it feels like the nickname was something like Monsa, M-o-n-s-a, the form of Mama, a form of Grandmother, Nana. It feels like it was Monsa, but I'm not sure. Her biblical name, her name at birth, uncertain. It feels like it starts with 'R', but I can't see clearer than that.

Understood?

DR: Yes.

#2 *Recording 10:42 Second Woman – Life and Incarnations*

DS: *Creator of All That Is, show me the second created female and her history journey into incarnations.*

This one was made when they left Eden. This one went south. It feels to us as if the first one went north. This one went south. This one did not have children until they were established beyond Eden. And then had many children over a quick period of time, two sets of twins. Feels as if there was a pregnancy a year, for eight or nine years, including two sets of twins.

In this family the memories were important; the ideas of Eden were strong. The purpose in this one, through her children, was to pass on what she remembered of Eden, because they did not. They had no memories or experiences of Eden, so she ensured that the memories were awakened in them and that they could remember an Eden that they did not know or visit.

She also existed for many years. Timeless realm held for a bit where they went to in the south; they managed to hold timelessness between the two of them. And so, it is hard for us to measure her years of living. But we would say that for every ten years she lived she aged one year. They could not prevent the aging, but they could slow it down.

When this one passed it feels accidental. A fall, rock slide, I cannot see, but it was an accident that involved rocks and harmed her brain that caused her death. She was not truly ready to leave, and at her deathbed there was some fighting and some resistance, but it feels to us as if the soul understood that this was no accident, and it was time. What was hardest for her to leave the body was to trust that the memories she had embedded in her children would hold. She was really attached to her purpose of keeping the memories of Eden alive.

This one was anxious to return to life, to incarnate again. But for the soul journey learnings and the soul journey expansions, time had to be taken. Again, there was a specific time that this one was to return and so it wasn't only her soul choice. It feels like there was some other plan at play at the soul level, at Creation level, so that this one would return at an opportune time. Again, her purpose in returning was to activate the memories.

Show me the lifetime please, show me as best you can where in the time lines, show me now.

This one came to the tribe while in Egypt, around the time of Moses but before the presence of Moses was really felt. This one was female again and she also had the memories from birth. This one was married young, thirteen. And her intention in her heart, her desire in her heart was to birth sons. And that was fulfilled. Feels like there were ten or twelve sons. But it feels like this one was not a name of importance. This was important in the tribe, the family line she was in and that she was, *zealous*

41

is too strong of a word, but very active in maintaining simplicity and in maintaining the memories of what had come before; of remembering who you are and what you stand for, she taught her sons. She was very active and alive, and lived a long time, and was very active in their marriages and arranging good marriages so that more sons could be born. She wanted to keep the memories and simplicities of the teachings of Eden alive, but more importantly she wanted to ensure the generations continued and that those teachings were held to them. She was a bit of a taskmaster with her sons to be sure they understood the importance of what she was teaching them. Some of the sons had the memories, some of them didn't, but they all took her learnings to heart, respected her, and loved her deeply. She was not harsh with them, but she was demanding; and she would not allow them to be disrespectful or forget the truth of simplicity. And so, she had an impact on the tribe, but in the simplest of fashions through her children, through her teachings.

#2 Recording 16:41 *Sons of the Second Woman*

DR: Were any of her sons people of note in the tribes in the Bible?

DS: *Following time lines, show me now please.*

We do not see any names of note. We sense a connection, many generations down to the apostle that was in the stories called Peter. But we cannot see with clarity to follow the connection. But we can sense in the one called Peter in your story that there was simplicity in his life, faithfulness in his heart, and it was passed down through the female of his line, grandmother, great-grandmother, and there were strong seeds in his heart of faithfulness that came from this one we are speaking of.

#2 Recording 18:32 *Third Woman, Life and Incarnations*

DS: *Creator, show me the third one and her journey line, soul journey. Show me now, please.*

This one was younger. It feels to us as if this was created at the age of thirteen or twelve. Womanhood began, but it took perhaps ten years of the timeless Eden-time for womanhood to begin within her body. There was a knowing that the other one created with her was her partner. There was camaraderie and friendship.

Feels to us as if this was quite deliberate on The Counsel's part to introduce a camaraderie of friendship, of relationship depth to this partnership. It was another experiment within an experiment.

This one likewise learned from the elder women. Very observant, very clear, questioning, understanding, taking things in quickly and she learned quickly. Understood purpose. Understood where she came from. And that is something she never forgot.

When the walls of Eden collapsed, this one was adult enough to leave with her partner on her own. They went southeast. They journeyed far, as if there was something driving them to be a little further away from the others. More independent, more separate. We see them in lush circumstances, almost jungle-like. And they kept to themselves. There were other tribes in the jungle they kept away from. It took them a while to establish themselves and they did not become pregnant until they were well established. They had a faithful routine within themselves as if they were holding their memories through some type of ceremonies that, over time, became religious.

In the beginning, there were ceremonies, gratitude, respect, appreciation of the Earth, of the animals, of their food, of their beingness, of their home. When this one fell pregnant there was great celebration, and it began a series of pregnancies. There was more acceptance, less directed intention, and so there wasn't the sense of her going to have daughters or sons. They were happy with the children. There was this sense of introducing a ceremony, that became somewhat religious as the generations moved on. But it feels like there were four generations that stayed in this settlement that they had initially set. It was the third and fourth generation that turned some of the first one's ceremonies into a religion.

There was great appreciation, great compassion, and patience with one another. Those were the teachings of the Eden that really held. The memories were not so important, though the female line did hold them stronger than the male and taught them. It was more the teachings, the way of living of Eden that wanted to be held. Memories did not seem as important to this group. How they lived, what they taught, how they treated one another, this was of the most importance.

When this young one passed, there were now four generations of her family that she had met, the fourth being very young. When she passed, it feels as if there was a rest of time in her soul journey. As if it was a long life, and when she passed, she was in need of rest. It was a laborious life, a hard life, but a happy one. And so, there was a sense of restfulness, and again, an idea that she would incarnate again at a specific time.

It feels as if this one incarnated not to the tribe again, outside the tribe, and waited quite a while. It feels as if this one, in the next incarnation which was hundreds of years, incarnated in the

Mayan culture of South America, female again, and brought some of this ceremonial religion, simplistic ideas with her. Feels as if she was an important figure in the Mayan culture. She was connected to a temple, but a female of recognition, a female of importance, a servant to the god or goddess of the temple. She did not have children in her first incarnation. But did incarnate again in the Mayans, and in that incarnation had children. She maintained her incarnations in the South American area for several generations. She brought something to those people, those Mayans, something in her DNA, something to those, that culture, to that strand of history. This be how we perceive the third journey. Does this answer your questions about this?

DR: Yes, it does, thank you very much.

Discussion

EVE

As I (Donna) channel, I am present to the information through my various senses, in many ways. This "post-channeling discussion" is a discussion at the end of each channelling session between Dan and me where I explain the visions, the understandings I am left with, and the knowings that remain with me in those first few minutes after the channeling is completed. What follows is that discussion.

#2 Recording 1:21: 45 Impact of Eve's Death on Men and Women

DS: Fascinating. I was so aware that horizontal and vertical, isn't the right word, but that's what it looks like. It is like the men stalled where they were and adapted, so they didn't grow any more after Eve, but the women grew. They (the women) took from Eve and they took that into the next generation.

DR: That's actually a good way of putting it, that the men stayed horizontal; spread out but it didn't persist long into generations. And with the women, it was vertical and deep, into the next generations. That analogy of the horizontal was exactly one that sort of made sense.

DS: And it is interesting because the fury at her death… Adam first experienced fury when his family was starving and that's the fury that we later see with Cain. But this was another level of fury. This was murderous fury. He was murderous. He murdered whatever animals he could find that were connected, like if it was a tiger… I didn't see what it was; it was a cat of some kind, large, very large, but the paws huge. He (Adam) killed every one he could find. He was murderous. He lost something. It was like she was his "sense". It is the only word I can find, his sense, his conscience. He lost that. He didn't know he didn't have it, until she (Eve) was gone. And then he had to change, and it took him years. Fascinating.

#2 Recording 1:23:30 Shame and Hidden Stories

DR: Interesting how the tribes kept information hidden that they didn't want to be known, that they were ashamed of. This happened several times in the stories. The same thing happened with the first Joseph, the same thing with Abraham and his son's sacrifice. They didn't want that murderous rage, that shame to be carried on in the stories. *(Note: This information is from Book 1.)*

This was well beyond my hope.

Here in the recording there is a pause. In that pause, Donna is reflecting on what Dan has said about the other stories. What is happening with Donna at this point is that the other stories are opening up in her memory and she can see the truth of what Dan has realized. Connections are being made and she can "feel" the truth of those connections. As that happens, those connections form a flow from "there" to "here".

These next words are Donna's expression of those connections as she "sees" them in the now time and understands how "then" and "now" are woven together.

DS: You know what's even interesting, just to add one more thing…

You're right, the murderous stories were shameful, and they were hidden. I can't help but notice *(in her vision of the connections)* that every story these days is filled with murder. There's no shame. Isn't that interesting?

That's what drives me nuts. There is not a lot of television I can watch because I can't watch despicable people do despicable things and get paid for it, get rewarded for it. I have such a problem with it.

But isn't it interesting that… you're right…consistently in the stories, murderous, shameful events… And it wasn't like there was a pride that they could not let Adam be seen that way. It was that this WAS NOT to be spoken. This was so shameful this was not to be spoken, and it never was. It was only witnessed by, I want to say, a dozen people, six men, ten men, six women.

Another pause in the recording as Donna "sees" the people who witnessed Adam's fury and understands what that means.

And so a mystery developed around her (Eve). I couldn't find what the mystery was, but it was like a lovely mystery that developed around the death of Eve. I couldn't find what the story was, maybe another time.

#2 Recording 1:25:34 Food and Clothes Provided in Eden

DR: Can you see about the food and things provided? Were these just dropped on the Earth?

DS: No. As I perceived it, it would almost be like living on a farm. The garden was there. I won't say hens, but the birds that laid eggs were there. And so, everything was at hand, but it wasn't like it was materialized out of some box. It was present to the land.

Here Donna is describing the vision she had. She is describing the farm, the supply of food on the "farm" type of space, as she saw or perceived it. Below as well, Donna is there and describing what she feels, sees, and understands from the residue left from the channel.

DR: Eden, and the walls, and the food, the birds, those are prepared in advance of Adam and Eve being placed there? It was already there?

DS: I would say it was, yes.

DR: You didn't see anything like it was being prepared in advance and then they (Adam and Eve) were just brought there?

DS: It did feel like The Counsel had taken care to create Eden.

They created Eden and then they deposited, *I do know that's the right word,* **deposited** Adam and Eve into Eden. But at first it was very impulse driven. They didn't eat three meals a day. They ate when they were hungry and when they were hungry, what they needed would be within reach.

DR: They didn't wear clothes?

DS: I would say they were draped. I never saw them nude. But they didn't change their clothes. If they had a robe, they wore the robe until it was tattered. Then, I don't know if another one was provided. I didn't see that, or if she (Eve) made one. I don't know.

But everything was there that they needed. I don't know... they never needed anything without it being provided because The Counsel made sure that what they needed was provided. I didn't see her (Eve) weaving thread or making garments. I saw them in robes, but it's not like they changed the robes every day.

#2 Recording 1:27:55 *Sin of Killing Healthy Animals; Eve Taking the Blame*

DR: Did they cook the food they had or eat it raw?

DS: Yes. I saw some raw and I saw some cooking. And the eating of meat, it wasn't forbidden, but they didn't crave it. I'm going to use a Catholic word, it was sinful.

That's why Adam's shame was so shameful when he killed that healthy animal, because the only animals they would eat were the animals that were weak or died; or those they came across that had been killed and then they would roast it. So, they might eat meat once a year, or twice a year. They didn't hunt.

I don't know if we made that clear. But it was so clear to me that the whole "original sin" thing was Adam killing a perfectly healthy animal because his family was starving. And it was a shameful thing to do. And the animal didn't know to be afraid, so it was victimized by that killing. But his family was dying and so... that was the sin.

DR: But that transferring the blame was incredible.

DS: Eve could feel how ashamed Adam was. She could reason to him that it was her and her children that he was killing for, so it was her to blame, because she was with child as well.

DR: So, she took away his sin.

DS: Isn't that interesting. She did, that's the perfect words, that's exactly what she did. That's exactly what she did. God bless you; those are the perfect words. She did and, and that became the story.

Still, I would like to find out why the apple, the snake, and the tree. I don't know if we can explore that another time because I couldn't find that. And what I'm doing this time when I hit, because there were several times when I hit real resistance from The Counsel. Part of this was The Counsel, part of it I don't know yet where it's coming from, that resistance. But when I hit real resistance from The Counsel, then that's when I use the words "Creator, if it's ready to be told, tell us", because I don't want The Counsel to decide what we can't know because they're still an incarnated being, and so that may be how we get to the apple, the snake, and the tree. Where did that come from? Why would they pick that? Was it just someone's imagination? Was it… I don't know. I couldn't find the link.

Above, when Donna speaks about there being a "resistance" to our knowing, to our questions, she is quite able to distinguish that part of the resistance is definitely coming from The Counsel. But she is unsure if all the resistance is coming from The Counsel.

When she refers to The Counsel as an "incarnated being" what she is referring to is that The Counsel is not infallible. They are beings that inhabit a dimension of time and space and are still experiencing lessons and learnings and so can, in their own way, interfere with what is told and what is not told. She is clear that she can feel another part of the resistance to our knowing coming from somewhere other than The Counsel, but she could not yet identify where that is. When she says, "I couldn't find the link", this is Donna trying to find the origins of the other part of the resistance and being unable to do so.

Donna is always aware of where the information she channels is coming from. That is important to her. But in this instance, she can sense the resistance, she can sense the resistance from The Counsel, but can also sense another resistance that she cannot yet identify the origin of.

#2 Recording 1:30:40 *Sin of Killing Animal, Not of Eating the Apple*

DR: Well, it was all kind of intermixed. In Eden, there was the Tree of Life which wasn't really a 'tree', but it was the biological materials. Then they (the storytellers) created the Tree of Knowledge of Good and Evil. Then today, the story we got about the animal being killed for food, it was all kind of tied together. These different stories tie together into one story about eating the forbidden fruit.

DS: When he (Adam) killed the animal, he was doing something, not that it was forbidden, but it was abhorrent. They didn't kill healthy animals. There was shame in him, but he overrode that natural instinct to look for the weakest animal, because his children were dying. There was cold and there were no greens and there was no option. He had no option. But it required a fury for him to do it. It was a shameful thing, and it was the first sin. I can see it being the first time they did something out of pure selfish need.

In the recording, you can hear the certainty in Donna's voice because she can see and feel the fury needed to do such a selfish thing. Donna's awareness of the "pure selfish need" makes her certain of what she says because she can "feel" the fury, she can feel the shame, and she can feel the need.

#2 Recording 1:31:53 Eve's Death Hidden

DR: So when I put in a question in my notes about the death of Eve, I just assumed it was kind of overlooked; that they forgot it, they did not know about it; it wasn't passed on. The other deaths, of Matriarchs, Sarah's death (Abraham and Sarah), Sarah's death was well-characterized, even to the place where she was buried. Yet Eve was forgotten about. So, I thought maybe they just forgot about it but then this whole hidden story came out, so it's like, "Oh my goodness!"

DS: Also, because she's tied to the sin of killing the first animal, the first killing. She is tied, you know, to the fury that Adam then experienced upon her death. She is tied to all that as if she was responsible for those shameful furies that he went into.

DR: I think many people, females especially, would be, let's say, "happy" to hear that the whole blame that Eve took as the first female, the blame for sin, was simply not true. And that's been a horrible mythology, to keep moving forward for forever. And that's one of the things that this book can do. It provides a different story. I think what I believe is that this is a true or truer story. At least it provides a better story, if not a truer story.

DS: And it seems more reasonable because I can say from how I experienced her (Eve), that she was almost childlike and innocent. Her soul was very new and there was a trust in her, and a kindness. She would not have seen this as a sacrifice for Adam. She would have been being kind to help his hurt and his shame that was so hurtful. I don't even know if I did justice to the language of the expressions that she went through when the emotional hurt was inflicted upon her. It was only because she was so innocent, and I almost wanted to use the word "pure" or inexperienced. As the emotional hurts and the emotional woundedness had started to develop in our race, she was really victimized by that. It was something that her soul, I won't say enjoyed, but her soul grew in the learning of, and the experience of, but as a human she struggled with that. It would be like someone being hypersensitive in an overwhelming place because this was a new development, this emotional hurt. It caused the women to come together because the women felt it more than the men did. It caused the sisterhood to form so that they could speak about it, because when she (Eve) tried to speak about it to Adam, he didn't understand what she was talking about. It really was maybe the beginning of the differences between male and female? It was fascinating. But the differences began because Eve was such a different soul. The Counsel intended males and females to be different.

#2 *Recording 1:35:36 Eve's Soul Chosen and Choosing to Incarnate*

DS: The Counsel chose her soul. I could feel that they knew what they wanted the soul to be, and those souls of that caliber were the ones who came. So, I don't know how that choosing happened, but it felt deliberate. It didn't feel accidental. Like they may have only wanted no memories, but then Creation perhaps interceded. I don't know what happens at that soul level. I don't know how those choices are made, but she (the soul of Eve) was very willing to come to this place, excited almost.

DR: Very brave too. Not just to be incarnated in a physical body on a planet, but to be the first of your line in a primitive place with no others like you around, except for Adam. To know what you are facing, that's impossible.

DS: And some of that I want to say was, and I mean the word kindly, "ignorance", because she never incarnated in such a way before. So that was a little bit of ignorance that she really didn't know, the soul didn't have an experience to reflect and say okay wait a minute we've been there before and do we want to do this again. There wasn't that imprint on the soul. The soul was really quite pure. Interesting.

#2 *Recording 1:36:55 Future Incarnations of Eve*

DR: I asked about the incarnations and that was at the end of my list, but I had to jump it up a lot more because they brought it up. That was so telling that she was supposedly the mother of Moses. So, she brought her experiences and knowledge forward to a very critical time.

DS: Yes. Deliberately so, and I could see her. I could see her so clearly. Dark-haired, small boned, determined, willful. But I could see it so clearly and very simplistic in her style. Like she wore the gold of Egypt, but she would wear one pendant. She wouldn't have bracelets. Or anything else. She was very simplistic in her style and very determined about her son.

She hid nothing. She was truthful, but she wasn't forthcoming. But she would never lie. She was very demanding on Moses, VERY demanding on Moses. Almost as if, on some level, she knew who he was.

I don't know that, but that's what it feels like. She was very demanding of him and that's the only other lifetime I can be certain of. I tried to find the first incarnation; it seemed connected to Cain's line but no, I couldn't find it.

There was a lot of resistance in The Counsel. The Counsel just doesn't want Eve not to be seen as the woman she was. They don't want her to be seen as something more than a human. Because she's like a baby factory. I want to say Eve was always pregnant.

DR: But Adam lived 930 years according to the Bible. Did she have 100 babies?

DS: Or 900 babies? No, The Counsel would not allow her to be seen as a baby factory.

DR: But you know the Bible does not have much about her at all. What they revealed to us was far more interesting, far more in-depth. The Bible has almost nothing about Eve. She is seen as just the created mate to keep Adam company, and she did the apple thing.

DS: The temptress and that's the end of her.

DR: So, this is marvelous information about her.

DS: Again, I'm shocked it's an hour. When you said, "Well, that's all my questions", I thought, "But we've only been channelling for 30 minutes; we can't be done." I love timeless realm; I just love it.

#2 Recording 1:15:10 Other Women of Eden

The Counsel and The 3 Other Created Females

DR: Well, it was a whole lot of information and new stuff so that I didn't intend to spend a lot of time with the previous chapter about Eve, but I wanted to do a couple of quick follow-up questions. At the very beginning I was asking about Eve and the other created women, the pairs, and that took a lot longer than I thought. It was actually fascinating and revealing about the other women. These are three other women key to the beginnings of the conscious human. So, I pursued that, because the information just came flowing out and it was absolutely wonderful. They're not women in the Bible, but they should be.

DS: They are women from The Counsel and there was deliberateness in their creation from The Counsel. There was deliberateness in the young one being so young. There was Counsel influence in those other three women. It almost was like the end of The Counsel's deliberate influence and so The

Counsel kept track of where those women went, kept track of what they became. There was deliberate Counsel presence with those three, whereas I'm not feeling Counsel presence with the other ones that you've asked about. I didn't feel any Counsel presence with Sarah nor with Rebekah. A witnessing, because of the importance of what established itself at Abraham, but not an interest in the females on The Counsel's part. So again, it feels like Creator is allowing me to be present to that time of Sarah, to that time of Rebekah, and witness what went on in that time as opposed to The Counsel showing me what they remembered. It's a very different feeling.

Section Two

MATRIARCHS

The following text was one of the first questions I (Dan) asked during a session for another book. The question arose because I was perplexed that the Matriarchs were given such a prominent place in the scripture, yet very little was written about them. What else did they do besides be betrothed to the Patriarchs? How did they function in the tribes? What did they think, feel, or how did they express themselves?

#1 Recording 33:28 (from Book 1) Role of the Matriarchs

DR: Just shifting a bit, just curious... in the biblical story of the Matriarchs, they're in the official Old Testaments, but there is almost nothing said about their role in the religion, in the spiritual tradition. I am just wondering if there is any information about the Matriarchs' role in the creation and continuation of the Hebrew religion.

DS: "The first thing we say to you is that the Matriarchs (Matriarchs speaking), "We stood behind; we accelerated the processes; we involved ourselves in the creations, but not in an obvious manner. There was fear, quite strongly, at that time, and **so we negotiated around the fear.** It is like someone participating in the orchestration of things from the back of the room rather than the front of the room. We did not require recognition and in fact made every effort that recognition would not find us. Our part was to soften, expand, and negotiate around the fears. This was an expanding time but the expansion sometimes created hesitation, uncertainty, and did aggravate the fears. There was a desire at this time to control the expansion, and so with the facade that there was control, the energy of the expansion was allowed. But we negotiated around so it seemed like it was controlled, but it never was. This is how we negotiated around the fear control stance. **Our job was to ensure the expansions, despite the control and the fear.** And standing in the back, out of the recognition light, we were able to do this with soft encouragements, soft praisings, and small insights. More often we provided questions, not answers, but the questions led to the answers that stepped around the controls and the fears of the times".

#1 Recording 37:16 Role of Matriarchs

DR: In part, now I am curious about the fears that would be limiting, and where those fears were coming from. Were these fears in the Patriarchs coming from internal or external sources?

DS: The fears... there was an awareness of change; there was an awareness of growth of mankind in the Patriarchs, and there was a caution that the growth not run like an unbridled stallion. There was a cautious sense of trying to direct the growth, which inadvertently, within the Patriarchs themselves activated control and fear, as if what started out as a cautious direction, nurtured itself into a fear. They did not originally have fear, but fear was created. There was this sense of too much too fast. There was this sense of always wanting to be certain of the origins of the growth, of the energy of the expansion, and then they became afraid when they were not so certain of the origins. There were all these energies weaving into one place and it was like the Patriarchs wanted to put a bridle on the stallion and direct it, which was all well and good, but as they started to direct it, control seeped in, and underneath that control were the fears that the energy was too much, that the expansion was too much. They were not certain of its origins. It was then that the Matriarchs *"stepped in because we could see the origins, could see the directions, and we were more confident of them than the Patriarchs were"*.

Does this make sense to your mind?

DR: Yes, yes, definitely.

DS: The sense is almost as if the Matriarchs are in the background seeing where the stallion is headed while the Patriarchs ride the stallion and try to control where it is headed. *"Because we could see where it was headed, we could assist without the fear"*.

Chapter Five

SARAH

Abram and Nahor took to themselves wives, the name of Abram's wife being Sarai and that of Nahor's wife Milcah, the daughter of Haran, the father of Milcah and Iscah. Now Sarai was barren, she had no child. (Genesis 11:29-30)

#2 Recording 25:37 Raising and Training of Sarah

DR: We wanted to talk about the Matriarchs in the Bible starting with Sarah.

You gave us previous information about her, can you expand upon that, her personality? First of all, how did she come to meet and marry Abraham?

DS: This one was very bright as a child, a little outspoken, clever; she questioned, wanted to learn. She found her way into the meetings of her father and the elders and questioned them of their studies. When she was young, she did this. She was young enough to be taken lightly and not offensively by the males. And so, her spark was recognized at a young age.

One in the circle of her father deemed her very worthy of his son. We want to say that her marriage was arranged when she was under the age of 5, 6 years old (*said surprisingly*) because the friend of her father recognized the spark within her and thought she would challenge his son and support his son well.

Her craving to have knowledge of the ways to live, it mattered to this one. It was never considered that she would be taught as the boys were taught, but it was admired that she wanted to learn. And so, she was betrothed to Abraham early. This was not Abraham's father; this was one of the circle of her father. But it was not the father of Abraham, it was the one who knew of Abraham and knew the mother of Abraham. And so, the idea of the betrothal was actually brought to Abraham's mother.

Again, Abraham was young, and it was at first rejected by her. Abraham was not faithful enough for such a wife in his young years. And it feels to us as if that betrothal for Sarah was held, in that Sarah was held for Abraham. But we want to say she was much older in her marriage to Abraham than was the norm. As if Abraham's mother was waiting for something in her son to appear, to let her know that he could be married to such a woman.

She befriended Sarah, trained Sarah as a woman. Without interfering with Sarah's mother, she added to Sarah's teachings those things that the men would not teach her. Sarah was educated for nearly ten years. Sarah was educated by the mother of Abraham, her own mother, and other very wise women. We want to say other very wise women was of the red tent. *(*This is a symbolic reference to the gathering of women to live separate, apart from the men, during their menstruation times.*)*

She was taught many things that most women would not have been. And there was a sense of her being prepared. Though the mother of Abraham would not know, or name, speak, what Sarah was being prepared for, there was a sense of preparation ongoing. It was accepted by all those concerned, and even with Sarah herself. For Sarah had already begun the visions. Her faith was deep and in her prayer space she had already begun to have visions. She did not share them at first with anyone. And then, as the teachings with Abraham's mother engaged, she shyly shared one. And from that, more teachings arrived.

Her visions were encouraged. Her prayer space encouraged. Though neither her mother nor the mother of Abraham understood the power in Sarah's prayer space, it was encouraged. They often prayed with her to keep her safe and ensure that the visions were of God, were of that which is right. By the time Abraham was ready for Sarah, she was well-developed. She was older than most wives would have been at marriage, near thirty when she was married. It does not feel like it was a young marriage, and she was well-educated. She could question Abraham and hold her ground with Abraham and help him to establish what he came to be. She held a faith with him and a faith in him, but she also challenged him; at times she found him wanting in his faith and would challenge him so. There were times it was deemed disrespectful by the men of Abraham and his circle. But Abraham understood her love as well as her faith. And a love did grow.

They did not fall in love when they were married, but a love did grow, and it grew from their faith. It also grew from shared memories for as Abraham accessed the memories, the prayer space of Sarah also deepened, and she had glimpses of memories as well. She was never really able to put full body to them, but she knew what they were and where they came from, and for her whole life she worked on strengthening and allowing more of those memories to come through. She knew of Eden, she saw it, she felt it in her memories. In her prayer space she worked to develop it quietly. It would not have been accepted by Abraham nor his circle that she did such a thing. But it proved very useful to Abraham as the decades moved by, because they became confirmation to one another. She could sometimes confirm what he had seen, feel the strength of his faith in what he had seen and encourage him in it.

There was power in her. There was voice in her. But there was great respect and a humble faithfulness. We would not call this one a sacrificial female, but she had power. It was, from The Counsel's perspective, intriguing to see her grow this way and to see her complement Abraham. We (The Counsel) had no interference with that and cannot state to where that graceful complement came from. But as we witnessed it grow, it seemed orchestrated to us, and we have yet to discover if it was orchestrated and by what or whom. We have no science to that.

These last statements are channeled from The Counsel directly, and from that we realize that much of the information about Sarah that has been relayed here has come through Donna from The Counsel's witness of Sarah and her growth. Interesting that The Counsel is "intrigued" by the sense of orchestration that surrounds Sarah, and yet they have no "science to that". Interesting to witness The Counsel and its limitations.

#2 *Recording 34:46 Sarah's Role in the Tribe*

DR: What was Sarah's role with the beginnings of the Hebrews?

DS: Her first influence was with the females. The second influence was with some of the males that were close to Abraham because they recognized her importance to him and how she nurtured his confidence and shared his faith. He, Abraham, offered her deep respect and so those close to him were obliged to do the same, when some of them would not naturally do so. But there was something in her that commanded that respect.

Her influence was with the females. She encouraged them to be stronger, to address themselves with more decisiveness, to be a little bit more in leadership, not leaders for that was not what the women were to be, but to be supportive of the leadership within their husbands, less subservient. She did not nurture sacrifice in the females that were within her influence and so she created a strength in the females of the tribe at that time. She demonstrated to them her support of Abraham in his weaker days, shared with them her belief in Abraham and shared with them demonstrations to show how her faith in Abraham, strengthened Abraham. She taught this to them so that it was something that was taught from the mothers to the daughters, to the granddaughters; that the women had an importance to be strong with the males of that time. They had an importance in the tribe; their strength strengthened the tribe. They were not subservient. They were not servants. They were active participants and acted in the faith, for she encouraged them in the prayer space.

There were not many who wanted to learn vision, to allow vision, but those that wanted to learn she would show. There was never one that had visions the way Sarah did, but they wanted to learn. Those that wanted to learn were taught. Not many wanted to learn, for there was fear of the visions in the females. They wanted to leave the visions to Abraham and to the men of the circle. But Sarah's influence was in strengthening the female role, strengthening the wife role in the marriage, strengthening the mother role in the family, strengthening and creating a role in the tribe itself. And then the influence with the males was more through Abraham. Sarah did not have direct influence, though she had great respect from them. They appreciated her role with Abraham and her importance to Abraham, and so they treated her with importance as well.

#2 Recording 38:13 Sarah, Half Sister to Abraham?

DR: Can you explain the story of Sarah being Abraham's sister or half-sister?

DS: By the time they came to this place (Egypt), Sarah had a role in the tribe, a recognized role in the tribe, and Abraham knew from his prayer space that they were to go into this place quietly and seemed to have no power, no threat. He needed to be perceived as an old man, small-tribe, uninfluential. And so, Sarah had to find a way to soften her way. She did not like it. She did not wear these years well. She had to secret her meetings with the women. She had to keep secret her visions, her strength. It would have drawn attention to the tribe. Though Abraham could not tell her why, he knew that it was important that attention not be brought to the tribe, that they blend in, melt away in a corner. These years were hard for her.

It was felt that the simplest way to do this was to be the sister. There were some traditions about the wives of the men, and though the men of the tribe did not like sometimes what was asked of their wives, because they needed to stay quietly unobserved in the corner, they did not fight when their wives were asked to perform service or servitude. It was deemed in Abraham's prayers, that if she was his sister, because he was the head of the clan, this gave her more respect than his wife would have achieved, and so sister she became. It did protect her. Some servitude was asked of her, some service was asked of her, but nothing that she was compromised in the doing of. None of the women were compromised or sacrificed, but their pride was injured, and it needed to be so. There were times that, through the women, they tested the men to be sure that there was no threat here. Each time Abraham saw the test coming, and they were prepared for it, and the husband of the wife was prepared for it, the wife was prepared for it. They saw it as an exercise to humble themselves and did so bravely.

DR: So biologically she was not his sister or half-sister?

DS: No. No, that would not have been tolerated.

#2 Recording 41:36 Sarah Giving Birth to Isaac at Elderly Age

DR: The story of Sarah having borne Isaac when she was old, like past menopause. This is a miracle. Can you explain that story please?

DS: We have already stated the marriage began at an older stage and at that time a bride of thirty or more years was unheard of. There were pregnancies in her fourth and fifth decades; two in her fourth decade, one in her fifth decade that ended in miscarriage. This was taken very hard by Abraham and by her, and there was much prayer around it. They feared it was a punishment for something.

In this next section, Donna is in the vision of Sarah and her aging and pregnancies. Often the words "it does not feel to us" are used to indicate that Donna is within the experience of Sarah and her life and observing. Donna then speaks of what she can sense from this space of observation.

We do not feel it was a punishment. It feels as if there was a deliberateness to her pregnancies and is if it was too soon for the one she was to birth. So, the body failed each time. This one was, we would say, close to sixty. It does not feel to us as if she was after menopause. But she was close to it. Sarah was thought of as a crone and unable to bear children. The miraculousness of it was that, although she was not menopausal, the ability to become pregnant and carry the pregnancy at this sixth decade stage, after the previous miscarriages, was miraculous to them.

This next section, The Counsel is relaying their observations of this situation with Sarah as it unfolded. They want to be clear that they did not interfere, merely witnessed this life unfolding with interest.

It feels deliberate to us as we witness this happen again. The Counsel had no interference and we watched this because it was unusual and there was a deliberateness to it. The body seemed different in this pregnancy as we witnessed it. The weaknesses we had seen in the forties and fifties were no longer present in the body as if the body had undergone a healing of some such that we never witnessed. The pregnancy was strong; the baby was strong, and was born with ease, and there was great celebration.

The source of information switches again here. Below, we are back to Donna being present in the observation and experience of Sarah's life. We are no longer in the observation of The Counsel, hence the words below "not from The Counsel". Donna is telling us she is no longer speaking from The Counsel's observation but from her own.

We would suggest to you, not from The Counsel, but we would suggest to you that as we witness this birth and feel ourselves present with her, that there was something divine about this birth. It was with ease, and her body responded beautifully. It was a "blessed birth" as the women would have called it. "A blessed birth" and this baby was blessed from the moment of first breath. This child was smart, quick, learned quickly, was strong in health, a bit demanding, but eager for life. And so, we do not see miraculous in that the conception was after menopause, but it was miraculous in her history of pregnancy and at her age.

#2 *Recording 45:20 Other Children of Sarah*

DR: Was this her only child?

DS: *Creator of All That Is, show me now please.*

There is a sense of a pregnancy. Isaac appears to us to be four or five years old. There is a conception and there is a pregnancy.

Creator of All That Is, show me now please. Is there a birth?

There is a birth, and it is a female and then we see no other conceptions after that.

#2 Recording 46:20 Daughter of Sarah

DR: Did this female survive?

DS: Yes, thrived, in fact. Was as strong as her mother, as willful as her mother, as smart as her mother. And was trained well by Sarah and had many of Sarah's gifts. Had even more of the memories than Sarah did.

DR: Was she born in Haran?

DS: We are not certain of where. We can say that Isaac was four, almost five years old.

Creator of All That Is, was this one born in Haran?

Donna asks the question again as a means of sharpening her focus and seeing vision of the answer. Seeking specific details does sometimes engage Donna's own doubts and requires more effort from her in her channel. Below, you can see that Donna does not succeed in reaching the level of detail that Dan is asking for.

I'm really not sure. I want to say no, but I'm really not sure. I can see the time frame but I cannot see the place.

#2 Recording 47:23 Daughter's Role with the Hebrew Tribes

DR: Did Sarah's daughter become an important person in the tribe?

DS: She did because in some way she carried on for Sarah. She worked with Sarah, trained with Sarah and then continued for Sarah. As Sarah aged, she continued with Sarah. And, then it feels as if she was at a certain point of training, and then Sarah encouraged her to leave. They did not need two Sarahs in this part of the tribe. She did join another tribe in marriage, and continued the teachings, the strength of females that Sarah taught; continued the importance of the wife to the husband that Sarah taught; continued the right of the female in pray space to know God. She continued and took it a little further. It feels as if it was a tribe that went further north, and it feels to us that when she left her family, she did not see her mother again in her life.

It was Sarah's doing, that she was betrothed and left. It was not what her daughter wanted; it was not what Abraham wanted, but Sarah saw it in her prayer space that it was important that the teachings go further than just where they were with her. And so, it was purposeful that Sarah arranged the marriage.

#3 Recording 14:29 *The Story of Hagar and Ishmael*

DR: Now we can continue with some of the biblical questions.

DS: You may proceed.

DR: We were talking about the Matriarchs in the Hebrew Bible starting with Sarah and Rebekah. I wanted to ask about the story about Sarah and her maidservant Hagar who the story says gave her maidservant to Abraham to bear a child and that became, I believe, Ishmael. Can you tell us about that story?

DS: Can we have the name of the servant again please?

DR: Hagar, H-a-g-a-r, Hagar.

DS: The first impression is that this is not true. Let me double check.

Donna, connected to the story/person of Hagar, feels the untruth of the story. In "double checking" she deepens her connection to explore what she can perceive, what is the truth, about Hagar and proceeds from there. Once in the deeper connection, Donna sees, and feels the character and essence of Hagar.

As we move more deeply into the Hagar essence and the personality, she is loyal, loving, and sacrificial. She has entered servitude with Sarah as a penance, wanting to be better within herself, recognizing some of her selfish traits and wanting to pay penance for them. She was drawn to the kindness of Sarah and wanted to emulate Sarah but failed miserably in her own mind. She was older as she entered the service of Sarah and so was not easily trained to service. It truly was an act of penance for her to be in service to Sarah. It did as she hoped it would; it broke the will of her selfishness.

When there was miscarriage of pregnancy with Sarah, Hagar offered to carry the child of Abraham if Sarah could not. Sarah objected, said no. There was discomfort, not as strong as jealousy in Sarah, but discomfort. She did not want to fail Abraham. There was concern, not as strong as a fear, but a concern that Sarah could not carry child to term. Feels as if we are before Isaac and this was when Hagar was considered, but Sarah objected. When I try to see Abraham with Hagar, I cannot see it. There is a sense of sin. There is a sense of disrespect to Sarah.

Our answer to you is what this child that Hagar bore was not of Abraham. It was told to be of Abraham but even that was objected to. This story was made, much after Abraham and Sarah had left this world, because it was strongly objected to. There is a sense of monogamy at this time within Abraham and Sarah, that could not allow it.

When we look to see where the child of Hagar comes from, it is connected to what we would call the right-hand man of Abraham. He was a holy man, a faithful man, and the child, the son that Hagar bore, was of this man. There was such closeness in Abraham's holy circle that this child was raised in the Abraham circle and came to be thought of as Abraham's son. We want to say to you that when the first idea of Hagar's child being Abraham's came to be spoken, it was malicious, spoken by those who had disrespect for Sarah and wanted to tarnish her in some way. It does not feel to be the truth. It feels like there was a monogamy of promise between Abraham and Sarah that would not be breached by such. The child was raised inside the inner circle, we shall call it, but it was not of Abraham.

#3 Recording 22:49 *The Story of Hagar and her Son Banished from the Tribe*

DR: So, the story that Hagar and her son Ishmael were then banished, left the camp?

DS: *Show me the time lines of Hagar and her son please, show me now.*

No. There was a time of leaving, but it wasn't banishment.

It feels like the holy teachings of this one is of Abraham's circle. It feels as if there were five in the inner circle of Abraham's teachings, the holy circle, and that two went off in different directions to spread the word. The remaining three stayed but there was no banishment. There was a leaving, but there was no banishment. Understood?

DR: Yes. So, did Hagar and son leave with the father of her son?

DS: Yes, they left as a family. It feels to us as if they went north when the other elder went south. They brought with them three other families to set up another settlement and expand Abraham's understandings of the original Eden ideas. Understood?

DR: Yes. Yes, that's fascinating.

#3 Recording 54:58 *The Teachings of Sarah*

DR: Can you summarize the teachings of Sarah?

DS: Very close to a view of equality, not quite to equality, but very close. That those of good heart who are dedicated to God could hear God's voice. It was VERY possible for females to hear God's voice and that they were to be strong, insightful and with opinion; not to tear down their husband, but a well-informed opinion to help support the husband. That when they came to wife and husband, it was a team not a servant to the master. It was the duty of the wife to be well-informed to support whatever her husband's business, whatever her husband's manner was. She was to support it, to know about it, to keep informed. Her husband was to present; her husband was to speak what the team knew. She was in the background but never less than the husband.

The women were to be educated, strong, and were to be close to their God, as close as anyone else. They were never less than. The only place there was not the strictest of equality was that any presentation to the tribe came through the male, not through the female. The females encouraged each other, taught each other, spoke to each other, presented to each other, but when it came to the tribe anything presented to the tribe, teachings, or decisions, always came through the male.

#4 Recording 1:22 Mother of Abraham

DR: Thank you. I wanted to go back and follow up on Sarah and some of the unanswered questions that arose. First of all, Abraham's mother, is her name known? Some sources say it was Amathlai, A-m-a-t-h-l-a-i, Amathlai.

DS: The naming of this one is a challenge because there was one name that named who she was and there was another name that she was known by. Almost as if one is a birth name and one is the name given to her under other circumstances.

"Show me the name that was spoken; please show me now." Donna uses the name as a way of connecting to the essence of Amathlai and as she does, she can sense the person, the essence and can then perceive the story of that life.

It feels to us as if the name that you have spoken, Amathlai, is the name she was known by. It actually feels that they're also circumstances where she was simply called Aman, A-m-a-n. It feels as if the Aman name was a loving affectionate gesture. But it does feel as if the name you have spelled is the name that she would go by. Understood?

DR: Yes. So, Abraham's mother, what was she waiting for in Abraham and so that he would be ready to marry Sarah?

DS: Abraham had strength and in the beginning his strength was a faith. We would call it a religious strength. The waiting was for this to partner within himself to his manhood's strength, so that he would be able, and we use the word deliberately, "able" to allow a woman as strong as Sarah to be his wife. It feels as if his mother was operating from a sense of knowing her son and knowing that he had to be at a certain level of maturity. She had great respect for her son, but she also saw his weaknesses very clearly. She wanted him to be at a place where there was more balance between the weaknesses and the strengths of him, so that his mind could allow for a wife as strong as Sarah. It feels as if his mother desired a wife as strong as Sarah. It feels as if his mother knew he needed a woman as strong as Sarah. But there was some resistance to Sarah's strength, particularly her leadership. It feels as if his mother understood Sarah and her leadership at a very deep level. It also feels as if it was God's gift to Abraham, but he had to be in a place where he was mature enough to accept it and enter the partnership with equality. This be how we would answer your question, are we clear?

DR: Thank you, yes.

#4 Recording 6:04 Sarah's Betrothal to Abraham

DR: Can you explain again who brought the idea of the betrothal to Abraham's mother? This was said to be a male in the circle of Abraham's father. So, who brought the idea of the betrothal to his mother?

DS: It feels to us as if this had a miraculousness to it. We want to say this man saw an image, or remembered an image of Sarah, in his prayer space. When he remembered Sarah, it was as if she had a halo around her head and this man felt that there was something holy about Sarah. This man already had a respect for what he perceived to be the Holiness in Abraham and he felt led to bring the two together.

This one was a teacher, or a Rabbi, or a holy man from the temple and had taught Abraham, so he feels elder to Abraham and more of Abraham's mother's generation. He perceived something holy within Abraham but like Abraham's mother, also recognized the immaturity and the little bit of rebelliousness within Abraham.

The rebelliousness within Abraham, as it matured, gave him determination and bravery but at the younger stages it was rebelliousness and willfulness. That is why the betrothal was brought to his mother, because the two of them agreed that Abraham had to, what word would we use, overcome, no, balance his rebelliousness with his maturity so that it could be a determined bravery. He needed to mature. He needed to grow up, grow into the strength of himself. This man who brought the betrothal is one who taught Abraham, who had visions in his prayer-space and saw these two together and had a vision of Sarah with a holy halo around her head.

#4 Recording 8:57 *Sarah Taught by Abraham's Mother*

DR: What did Abraham's mother teach Sarah, while Sarah was growing up?

DS: The first part of the question again.

DR: What did Abraham's mother teach Sarah?

DS: Abraham's mother was, they would have called her holy in those days. She had awareness and insight and she recognized a strength in Sarah. She witnessed Sarah's mother trying to tame her and she would use that word deliberately. She witnessed Sarah being tamed and she understood the importance of what was being tamed out of Sarah. And so, she actually asked to be part of Sarah's upbringing. Abraham's mother was seen as Aman (her name) and she was respected and so it was a great offering that she paid any attention to Sarah. This was an honour, and so Sarah's mother would never have said no. What she taught Sarah was how to be willful without dominance. How to be clear in her prayer space. How to hear God's word in her prayer space. How to respond to God's word. And then the practical relayance (to relay) of that. How to speak to men of what she has heard from God's word, without making herself appear equal or as more than them. How to hold her space but hold it with power, strength, and bravery. Bravery within Sarah, she (Abraham's mother) was particularly careful to nurture the bravery without creating a warrior; to nurture intelligence without creating arrogance; to nurture willfulness without losing compassion, patience, compromise. Abraham's mother taught Sarah how to be a different woman than would have been recognizable in the times. This be what Sarah was taught.

#4 Recording 12:05 Role of Sarah's Mother

DR: So, Sarah was also educated by her own mother? Is there a name for her own mother?

DS: Sarah was not educated by her own mother. Sarah was tamed by her own mother. Her mother wanted her to be the docile wife of someone of importance. She wanted her to be obedient and not have thoughts of her own. And so, she taught Sarah the skills of running a household, of keeping the household in order, how to be head of the household. But the very things that Aman (this refers to Abraham's mother) wanted to draw forward in Sarah, her mother wanted to suppress.

Can we get a name or position for Sarah's mother please? Show me now.

It feels as if the family of Sarah was a good family recognized in the tribe for their effort. Her father was recognized for his integrity and his work ethic. It doesn't feel like her father was a commander in any way. He was involved somehow in the circle that helped to make decisions for the tribe. He could not be called a chieftain or any some such. The only name we can see connected to the mother is Nanosite, N-a-n-o-s-i-t-e. It feels like a first name shortened to Nan, but I am not certain.

#4 Recording 14:54 *Lineage of Sarah's Mother and Father*

DR: What is the background or lineage of Abraham's mother?

DS: It was a strong and respected lineage. It feels as if her qualities came from her father's side and the lineage came through the father. There is strength in the father's line, reverence, and obedience to the Lord in her father's line, service to the Lord in her father's line. There are three generations; her father, grandfather, and in her great-grandfather's generation there was experience of miracles. There was a strictness in her father's line, adherence to the teachings of the previous generation. When we follow the generational line, there is more Holiness at the great-grandfather stage. Sarah's father being generation one, there is Holiness and miracle at two generations back, the great-grandfather. Then there is another holy and miraculous experience three generations before that; five generations before Sarah's father there is a continuance in that generational line of faithfulness and adherence and obedience, and an ability for visionary. We do not say there are prophets in this line. But there are those who knew God's word in their prayer space and could have been prophets but chose to be in service instead.

It feels like there are names that start with "J", and it feels like a similar name was given several times. I don't know if it's Jacob or John, but it starts with a J and it feels like every second generation had that same name. It feels like Sarah's father name began with the letter "J".

This be the best I can give you, understand?

In this last section, Donna is trying to see the details of the names which is not often easy to see. In not being able to see the names clearly, instead Donna speaks to what she can see with certainty. For Donna, the deeper the level of exact detail, the more she sometimes struggles with her fear of being wrong.

#4 Recording 18:25 Abraham's Family Residing in Ur

DR: Was Abraham and family living in the city of Ur?

DS: They were first in a quiet place, not hiding exactly, but in a quiet village near Ur. They would visit Ur, or they would go to the markets of Ur, but they didn't live there. There was this simplicity in the living. Abraham's father wanted some solitude. It would be equated to someone living in the country instead of the city, though that is an oversimplification. Ur was not what would you call the city in your day and time now, but it was still busier, more people. As Abraham reached youthful manhood, there was a sense of movement to Ur for education, temple, there were reasons pertinent to Abraham's upbringing. It doesn't feel like his family lived there; he moved there. Then there were connections to the tribes; there were connections to the teachers, religious connections, spiritual connections, and it did become his home. When he created his family with the marriage of Sarah, he stayed there. It feels as if he moved his mother there after his father's death, out of duty, out of love. We can say yes to your question.

#4 Recording 20:52 Sarah and Her Family Residing in Ur

DR: So, Sarah and her family were from the same area in Ur or nearby?

DS: Abraham's father's home was west of Ur and Sara's family's home was east. Unlike Abraham's father, they were not in the country and solitude. They were perhaps in a small village, not as big as Ur is, but it still would be called the village. It wasn't isolated. They did come to Ur for certain celebrations.

#4 Recording 21:56 Abraham's Education in Ur

DR: So, there was a temple in Ur that Abraham went to? What kind of religious practices were there?

DS: It was for education, that the elders held meetings not classes. Meetings for the young men to help them find their way, find their place in the tribe. There were prayer times, where they would pray together, the prayer space of vision. Those young men that were adept at the vision space of prayer were taught more often and Abraham was one of these. These were not the elders that would have allowed the women to be taught or even recognized as having visions in prayer space. This was done quietly among the women themselves.

Abraham was chosen and educated but it was like meetings rather than classes. There was strictness, expectations, and many rules. Abraham did struggle with the rules. But he did see improvement in his visions and a stronger sense of God in his heart and so he obeyed, because he found results. Once he became his own man, he did change the rules, for some of them did not make sense to him, and did not seem to improve situations.

DR: So, this school was taught by people like the Hebrews? They didn't worship the local gods?

DS: No, this was the Hebrew elders and the elder they were, the more status they had in the teaching. They were maintaining the beliefs, maintaining the history, maintaining the stories. Abraham was not a storyteller, because his visions took him another direction, but these men also trained the storytellers.

#4 Recording 24:53 What the Hebrews Called Themselves

DR: If this was before the Hebrews were established as a name, what do these people call themselves?

DS: There is a smile in the response to this. The Counsel is present and wishes to speak that the names then were more connected to the families. There was not that much identity yet to give themselves a name. They were of the name of their father. The naming, we speak to of it because it was interesting to witness how naming grew in the tribe and what naming became. There was only identification to the family line in the time of Abraham. But that we (The Counsel) did watch evolve, until it became the naming of the tribe and then the naming of the land, and then the naming of, the naming of.... It was interesting to witness how important naming became as mankind evolved. And so, there is a smile at your question because The Counsel would say this was before the time of naming. They would want to be known as men of God, families of God, and there was not a sense of naming yet.

#4 Recording 27:10 Beliefs of the Elders

DR: So, these tribes were teaching about the same beliefs that Abraham had. They were teaching him about one God and the whole belief system?

DS: They were perpetuating the Eden beliefs. They were perpetuating the simplicity, the honour, the integrity, but it was also starting to expand as we have spoken of before. Evolution had influenced the growth and it influenced the faith and had influenced what prayer space was becoming. So, our interest (the interest of The Counsel) was there because of the influence of the evolution. There is a sense, and we (The Counsel) traced it, of a continuous growth in beliefs and we began to see evolution's influence on the beliefs, and we watched it grow. It was about how to live; how to serve God; and this was the beginning of what God wanted in service. This was near the beginning of the rules. The rules first showed themselves in the meetings with the elders. **There was a desperateness in the elders to maintain the history through the family lines and the rules came from that.** We are saying the dance, the weaving between evolution and the beliefs and holding the history, we (The Counsel) could monitor it. It was as if we could see the weavings of strings, weaving into new directions.

#4 Recording 29:29 *Death of Abraham's Father*

DR: One of the Bible stories says that Abraham's father, Terah, died in Haran and not in Ur as you seem to say?

DS: Abraham's father did not die in Ur. He (Abraham) moved his mother to Ur after his father's death. *Accessing, show me the time lines and the story lines here, show me now.*

We are going to suggest that there was travel and that Abraham's father died in his travels. We cannot be certain of the place that Abraham's father died, but it was not at home. When his father travelled, his mother came to Ur to stay with Abraham and one trip his father did not return. I'm not even certain that the body was returned.

Was the body returned? Show me storyline, show me time lines now please.

The body was returned, but it took a while. There wasn't certainty of his identity and until someone could be certain of his identity, and it wasn't until that identification had happened that the body was returned to Abraham in Ur. So, we will say that his father did not die in Ur, that he died elsewhere, but we cannot name the place.

DR: Is it known how he died?

DS: *Show me the time line, show me the events, show me now please.*

It feels accidental. The body looked beaten, but it was accidental. The chest was crushed. There were marks on the chest. By the time the body was recovered to Abraham, they did not know what had caused the marks. It feels to us as if it was an animal or horse or something heavy crushed the chest. He died from that injury.

#4 Recording 32:14 *Marriage of Sarah and Abraham*

DR: So where did Sarah and Abraham get married? Was it in or near Ur?

DS: This is important. There was an importance put upon where this marriage would be sanctified. It feels as it took place on his father's land outside of Ur. It was ceremonial and greatly celebrated, but it wasn't a party. It was sanctified. It was ceremony. It was at his mother's insistence that **this was not a party. This was a beginning of something that was Holy and needed to be Sanctified and taken with Reverence.**

It was an outdoor ceremony on his father's land, and it was after the father's body was returned. It was part of the entitlement recognizing Abraham's next stage of manhood. It was a sanctified, reverent ceremony. There was a sense of Holiness to it, and it feels like that was unusual. Ceremonies of coming together in marriage and partnership were more celebratory, but this was different, and it was all his mother's creation.

#4 Recording 34:15 *Officiating Sarah's Wedding*

DR: Who officiated this wedding?

DS: It was the elders. There were three of the elder teachers, male. It was unusual in that Abraham's mother asked them to pray and asked about the sanctification that was important, the sanctification of this marriage. It started something different. It involved God in ceremony in a way that was not the norm. It was the three elders who prayed and created the sanctification ceremony, and it was at Abraham's mother's insistence or request.

#4 Recording 35:09 *Sarah's Daughter and Her Life*

DR: Sarah had a daughter, I believe, after Isaac was born. Where was she born, in Canaan?

DS: Definitely near Canaan. I can't tell if it was in Canaan or on the travels to Canaan, but we could say yes to Canaan.

DR: Then when this daughter left home and was asked by Sarah to leave home, how old was she at that point?

DS: Fourteen, end of the thirteenth year, beginning of the fourteenth year, around the birthday of the fourteenth year. There was ceremony with this as well. It was symbolic of her stepping into the next stage of her life and there was a ceremony of leaving childish things behind.

DR: The tribe she married into, were they a Hebrew tribe or like a Hebrew tribe of the same faith?

DS: Yes. Sarah would not have had it any other way. It was to bring the attitude that Sarah had taught her daughter to another place, further away, quietly among the women. Her daughter excelled in strength, right mindedness, clarity. She was not so strong in the visions of prayer space, but she understood the visions of prayer space and could help to instruct those women that were good at it.

DR: So how far away did she live from her mother and father?

DS: Two days travel; one day, one night, second day, a second night arriving there the morning of the third day.

DR: I think it was said that she went to the north?

DS: They started out east, following the sun and then moved to the north, yes.

In the answer above, when Donna is counting the days. She is doing this because in her vision, she can see the daughter's travel and so is counting the sunrises and sunsets to answer the question. And again, in the reply to direction, Donna lifts into a higher view of the vision to "see" the direction the group travels and then comes to the reply. It is why this is not just a "yes" or "no" answer, but rather a detailed one. Donna is speaking from what she is witnessing in her vision, not from knowing.

#4 Recording 38:36 Daughter's Relationship with Isaac

DR: Was Isaac also born in or near Canaan? What was the relationship between Isaac and his sister?

DS: Relationship with the sister was difficult. Isaac, like his father, was willful and rebellious. What added to the difficulty was the status of Abraham. There was more arrogance in Isaac, and he did not want to be equal to his sister. There were disrespecting squabbles with his mother and his sister which were punished, severely.

Abraham recognized the youthful ardour and rebelliousness in his son and did seek to direct it, redirected it, but it was more difficult with Isaac. This did change later after the experiences Isaac shared with his father. But in regards your question, the relationship with the sister and the brother was difficult. There was some pettiness and jealousy. There were things that the sister excelled at that Isaac did not and there was relief in the family when the sister left.

#4 Recording 40:28 How Often Did Sarah See Her Daughter?

DR: So, this sister, did she ever see any of her family again?

DS: She saw her mother on certain ceremonial occasions, maybe every two or three years. It wasn't annually or every few months. Every three years, there was a gathering that several family tribes came together for every third year, and that was when she renewed connection to her mother.

DR: So, she stayed close to her mother?

DS: No. But she was able to renew with her mother at these ceremonies, to bring to her mother her doubts, her concerns with how to teach what Sarah wanted taught. But we would not say that there was closeness, no. It was like Sarah was always with her in that there was often the wonder of what would Sarah say, how would Sarah handle this, what would Sarah say to this teaching. But for the most part, this was important that the daughter find her individual independent strength, and she did achieve that. These were not women who were dependant on one another.

DR: Did the daughter ever resent being pushed out, asked to leave?

DS: There was fear in the journey away, for those childish things that brought a comfort she was not allowed to carry with her. There was anger and fear. But in less than a year, she recognized her position and grew into it quite beautifully, so we would say no.

DR: Did she have a good marriage?

DS: Yes, she had a good marriage because she was a good wife and her husband appreciated the strength of his wife, the goodness of his wife, and it was a good marriage.

#4 Recording 42:43 Sarah's Name Change

DR: Why does the Bible have Sarah's name changed? At first it was Sarai, S-a-r-a-i, and then S-a-r-a-h. Sarai to Sarah. Is there a reason for that?

DS: It is a language difference. We are going to suggest that the first stories of Sarah were written by someone different than who wrote the later stories. It was a language pronunciation. The language was slightly different in dialect and so it created a different spelling. It was more that whoever wrote the story, spelled it the way they heard it – Sarah – and then the second writer again spelled it the way they heard. It wasn't a deliberate change of name.

#4 Recording 43:43 Abraham Name Change

DR: So similarly, in the Bible, Abraham's name was changed

from Abram to Abraham. Can you explain that?

DS: How do you spell the first name?

DR: A-b-r-a-m. Abram, to Abraham.

DS: There are phonetics involved here as well, but there is something else here.

What is the story line, show me now.

There was another with a similar-sounding name to the first name, and so Abraham was created to make the distinction. It feels like this was after they left Ur, and Abram was the only Abram in Ur. But where they went to after that, there were others with similar name. Abraham was not a common name; it was a created name to differentiate Abraham from the others.

#4 Recording 45:22 Similar Tribes in the Vicinity

DR: So, where Abraham and Sarah lived, in Canaan, were there other Hebrew tribes in the vicinity, similar tribes, similar beliefs?

DS: Yes, they were quietly discovered. They found each other through trading, through working. But these were quieter. There was some status around Abraham that made some of the other families only very quietly friendly with them, as if they do not want to draw attention to themselves, and Abraham did draw attention.

They held similar beliefs for the most part. There were three generations. They were smaller families, but they had not come to what you would call a tribe yet. They feel as if they are small families that moved in this direction and then found a place to settle, were happy to find others of like mind, but did not band together. They wanted to be quiet in their life, simple in their lives, and it feels like there was never more than three generations in them.

DR: So where did these family groups come from?

DS: That is hard to say. It feels like there were five families, and they came from different directions. It doesn't feel like any of them knew each other when they arrived here. It feels like three of them had lived nomadically and had decided to settle, which brought them to the Canaan area. The other two have been in Canaan longer, perhaps for four generations, but there were still only three generations alive.

#4 Recording 47:49 *Abraham's Teachers in Canaan*

DR: What brought them, as well as Abraham and Sarah, what drew them all to Canaan?

DS: Growth, desire to know more, desire for experience. They were not missionaries in any way shape or form. It was about life experience; it was about life opportunities, and it was about learning. It feels as if there were educators or men of wisdom in Canaan and specifically for Abraham, he did seek out more learning and so sought to find elders wherever he heard of them.

DR: So, he heard that there were elders, teachers in the land of Canaan and so was drawn there?

DS: Yes. There were very positive experiences from his education meetings as a young man and as he grew and watched change in the families around him, he craved more wisdom. So, there were times he even spent time with elders that would not be called Hebrews, would not have the same faith, but had the experience of wisdom in life. So, he was not always quick to identify himself, but as a man of learning only.

DR: So, the elders who taught him in Ur, knew of these other teachers in Canaan?

DS: No. No. Abraham heard of them from travelers and there was concern because they were not always of the same beliefs. But Abraham was clever, and his intellect was recognized which is why he became known and stood out more than the other families would have liked. And so, he was respected for his intellect and discussions, philosophical discussions, faith discussions. He entered into even with those of different faiths, but he entered into them gently, without forthright zeal, but more to listen and to learn, and it increased his wisdom greatly.

Again here, Donna describes the visions she is seeing of Abraham in the circles of discussions. She can sense the challenge they presented to Abraham. She can feel the differences in faith and how that created discussions. She can also sense Abraham and how he embraced these differences in order to learn. Donna can feel the need within Abraham for "wisdom" not just knowledge. These responses are coming from a witness of these discussions and the feeling of Abraham as he grew within these circles. There is such a sense of the man Abraham did become, starting here.

DR: So, once he arrived in Canaan, Abraham sought out these wise men, these teachers?

DS: Yes. They had meetings. I don't know how to call them.

They weren't classrooms. They weren't prayer services. They were meetings, discussions, where they discussed the way of living, the way of deciding, the class structures, the developments, and the implications of the developments. They were elders who had seen great change and discussed the event of those changes and the results of those changes. Abraham was of interest to this.

DR: What was the lineage of beliefs if they were different?

DS: I cannot see the lineage of the beliefs, but the main difference was in service to God and in that which is connected to what we would call the visions in prayer space. These men were not supportive of visions in prayer space. There was fear of that and so that was kept quiet by Abraham.

They had similar beliefs, but there was more strictness and more fear in them, but they were still supporters of simplicity. There was more fear about invention. There was more fear about the changes. It feels as if Abraham was more supportive of the changes. Abraham, although we are using the words of The Counsel, Abraham, he was more supportive of evolving, but Abraham would not call it evolving. These wise men in Canaan were not. So, the discussions were how to keep the life with honour, how to keep the life of simplicity. And, the strictness, they were far stricter, but they had seen things Abraham had not. They had witnessed invention and Abraham wanted to understand what the history had shown them and so he was a great listener of their stories. He only asked simple, pointed questions. He shared very little of his own experience and this catered to the ego of these men, and so they did not need to know of him. They liked the adorative place, that reverence, that Abraham had for their experience.

It does not feel like he did this for a long, long time. He did this with specific purpose and then, I don't know how, but then his presence there finished without them ever really realizing that the very things they were frightened of, Abraham practised, such as the visions in prayer space, the idea of talking to God.

DR: So, what happened to them and their beliefs? Did they disappear?

DS: No. Their beliefs hardened; their beliefs strengthened, and the fear strengthened as well. They became punishing, strict. It feels as if they also entered into the ruling of the city, as if there was somehow a connection between the rulers and these wise men; as if they somehow helped the rulers hold order. It wasn't clear the difference of state and religion. It was the wise men ruling the city. So, they became part of the rulers of the city, the organizers, those that kept the city organized and at peace.

#4 Recording 55:01 Conflict Between Hebrews and Canaanite Elders

DR: Did the Israelites end up fighting with these people, their beliefs?

DS: We would say yes to that, but it doesn't feel like that happened in Abraham's time. I'm not certain of that, but we can say yes to the question.

#4 Recording 55:33 Unnamed Women Contributors from Adam to Abraham

DR: One last question. In the lineage from Adam and Eve to Abraham and Sarah, very few women, especially wives, are even mentioned in the Bible. Were any of these women contributors to the tribes, to their beliefs, to their training? These women who have not been named, from the time of Adam to Abraham?

DS: Yes. There were very specific women, more often recognized at the elder stage, when the daughters were married, and the grandchildren appeared. This is when the grandmothers were safe to speak of things that hadn't been spoken. With each generation more was spoken, and it was spoken sooner... so that Sarah, one, two, three, four generations before Sarah, the mothers and grandmothers began to speak sooner. They speak to the daughters sooner, before they became the wives. More recognition was given among the women from the women, and it started to develop into something that became acceptable, acceptable is too strong of a word, tolerated by the men. So that by the time of Sarah, recognition began, and the men could see the purpose to an intelligent and strong wife.

I don't know how to say this... from Eden, from Adam ¬ Eve, three generations after Eve, is when things started to change, and the women became quieter. They didn't lose Eve's teachings, but they became quieter about it and often did not speak until they felt they were elder and had earned the right to speak.

Then the elder grandmother spoke, *I'm going to say four, I don't know how many generations.* The elder grandmothers would speak near their death moments, and share stories and wisdoms and visions. That ignited something in the daughters of the grandmothers that allowed them to speak to their daughters, the granddaughters. The grandmother would speak to her daughter around the time of her death which would ignite in her daughter, who is now a mother, to speak to her own daughter sooner. So, there was a time where it was held and then it faded quietly and then it became renewed again. So, there was a movement. If there would be women named, they would be named as the grandmothers and so it almost seemed like it was every third generation, but it wasn't. It was in all the generations, but it was only when the woman was at the grandmother stage close to death, that it was spoken and recognized, recorded, listened to.

DR: So, there was a passing on of knowledge, of education, of wisdom?

DS: Of visions of what was not wrong, of what was allowed, of what was true, of what could be experienced, of how women could know God differently. How women could be in their own kind of power, though the word power would not be used. An acceptableness of how women were. What they knew and the simplification, and the vision and the connection through their children and the intuitive awareness as a mother. There were things that the grandmothers made acceptable, but it was most often made acceptable to those that were mothers, because it started with the care of the children, with the birth of the children, and the awareness you had of your children and so the grandmothers would speak to their daughters about their children, their grandchildren.

Their daughters were mothers now and they would understand what the grandmother said, because through becoming a mother, they had experienced similar things. It was through the childbearing and through the raising and understanding and keeping the children safe. And then there was a time where then it became spoken from the mothers to the daughters long before they became mothers and it started to develop into something else. But it was all done very quietly, not that it was hidden, but it was easier to be quiet with it and under-spoken with it, soft with it, not challenging with it.

It wasn't about power. It was about how to keep your children safe. How to be strong for the family line. How to protect the family line. How to know things for the family, for the husband, for the fathers. It wasn't about power. It was about how to live and how to listen as you lived, that kept the children safe and kept the families safe. And then as that strengthened, by the time of Sarah, it became something more taught, and more encouraged and also more recognized by those men that were ready to have such a partner.

DR: So, it seems it was less of a formal training of mother to daughter or granddaughter but more of a sharing of their experiences with their daughters or granddaughters.

DS: It began as the grandmother teaching the daughter, who is now a mother, how to keep her children safe. How to keep her family fed. How to look after her family. It came through the mothering first and then later it started to be beyond the mothering, and more connected to the faith and service of God. Understood?

DR: Yes, yes. That's beautiful, thank you very much. I think that's all I have for questions for today.

Discussion

SARAH

Sarah Started the Strength of Women

DR: You didn't hear what I heard come through today. It was absolutely amazing.

DS: OK, well you need to keep telling me that. And that's what David (Donna's husband) said. David said, "Hon, you're a professional. You've been doing this way too many decades to worry about this." But I do.

DR: And it's exactly what I had hoped for and more in what you're able to pull out. In this case, the women and their personalities and their feelings and their needs and wants, and what they were. I didn't want to have like a travelogue, like a mechanical thing: here is Sarah, she is the mother of so-and-so. I wanted the depth of the person. I wanted it to be oriented about women for women. It's wonderful; it's wonderful.

DS: Sarah started in the Hebrew tribes, the strength of women. She started that we are strong for our men, but we are strong.

DR: And that's not in the Bible.

DS: She started that; she encouraged those women to have prayerful visions, to have journeys. There weren't too many who were brave enough to do it, but if anyone wanted to, then she helped them. She recognized independent spirit and encouraged it, but also taught them how to do it that was supportive of the husband, not dominant of the husband. So, she really started that strength in the female line.

DR: Not only are these women all in the Hebrew Bible, but there's also a specific prayer that is said every Sabbath in the synagogue. There is one prayer specifically that is said a lot and that is about Abraham, Isaac, and Jacob (the three Patriarchs), and Sarah, Rebekah, Rachel, and of course, along with Rachel, Leah, also a wife of the third one. So, there is actually a prayer about these four women, so they're important, but there's nothing said about their importance, *nothing* said. But if they were just a wife, why are you bothering to mention them?

DS: No, they were not just a wife. Sarah was allowed to become what she was because at the age of three, four, and five, would intrude upon the elders meeting with her father and sit there and ask questions of the elders. Because she was cute and young, they let her get away with it. If your 12 year old girl had done that, she would have been ousted by the seat of her pants, but she got away with it. It started her, it sparked her, and then as she grew, she became respected. As the wife of Abraham, she was respected. There was a recognition that all that Abraham was did not only come from Abraham. There was a recognition that Sarah had a part in that. Now they wouldn't have taken orders from Sarah, but they would never have disrespected Sarah, because it was demonstrated by Sarah the importance the wife could be. Then she taught other women to be that important, no matter how lowly your husband was, to be that important. That was like the beginning of this powerful woman that would not have been given power by the elders of the tribe, would not for a moment, but because it came the way it did, because it started with Sarah in the circle of the elders with her father, it was, what's the word I want, allowed because she was cute and she was silly and she probably didn't understand anyway, but that just triggered her into intelligence growth. Then, because she kept that growth up, and then, because she was given to Abraham, she just was respected. I would bet that if something happened to Abraham she would have been listened to, you know. It was interesting. She started something.

#2 Recording 1:12:04 Matriarchs

Sarah Giving Birth at Older Age

DS: It was thought to be so because her body wasn't the same body that had miscarried before. Her body was stronger. It was...I don't know how to ask how to identify this, because it's not The Counsel, but there's something at play here. There's something divine, dare I call it divine, at play here that's really orchestrating what is brought to the planet.

#4 Recording 1:13:59 Matriarchs

Role of Women Becoming More Active in the Tribe

DS: But don't you think that part of that could be technology? That there were storytellers for a long time and there was a time, if I remember correctly my history, where writing was very expensive and it was done by a very select few at very select instances, and so there simply could be nothing malicious, but that the stories were lost? And particularly the females' because they were just looking after their families. They didn't know what they were creating and becoming. As I perceive it, they were just looking after the families, looking after the children, as every woman of the time did, and then once it started to come forward around Sarah's time, to be an actual teaching, of preparing the daughter to be a wife, that's when it starts to be more. I think that's why Sarah comes into the writings, because Sarah was different. Sarah's service was going to teach women. It wasn't just grandma and mama telling me what to do and be ready for sex on the wedding night, this is how you feed, how you get a baby to attach to the nipple. This started to be more than that in Sarah's time. It started to be a partnership that listened to the family members and listened to the tribe, and kept Abraham informed and confirmed Abraham's visions, and had visions of her own and helped. So, there was almost like, she became like another type of female chief to the tribe. That hadn't been that way before. Before it was, as I perceive, just mothers and grandmothers looking after the family line, because the family line was the original tribe.

#4 Recording 1:15:55 Matriarchs

Sarah's Wedding as New Spiritual Beginning

DR: Right, but when you described the wedding it was a key moment. It was a spiritual beginning, an initiation of something new and different. Two people who had very strong faith coming together to create something was a key.

DS: It was. I didn't see Sarah's mother, but Abraham's mother had a vision of this and she could see who Sarah could be. She saw Sarah and she agreed with whomever it was that saw Sarah in a vision with a halo around her head. She understood the Holiness of Sarah and that Holiness had to be recognized in this partnership. This wasn't just a celebration, it was a changing point in the ceremony of what marriage was, what partnership was. It wasn't just joining us anymore. It wasn't joining to perpetuate the family anymore. It was more than that.

Chapter Six

REBEKAH

Abraham said to his senior servant "...go to the land of my birth and get a wife for my son Isaac." (Genesis 24:4)

Then Laban and Bethuel answered, "This matter is decreed by the LORD, we cannot speak to you good or bad. Here is Rebekah before you; take her and go, let her be a wife to your master's son as the LORD has spoken." (Genesis 24: 50-51)

#3 Recording 55:24 Rebekah's Betrothal to Isaac

DR: The story of Rebekah's betrothal to Isaac, was this an arranged marriage?

DS: To keep the name straight, this is Isaac of whose father?

DR: This is Isaac, the son of Abraham.

DS: She (Rebekah) objected to it at first. She did not want to marry. But she respected Sarah, and when Sarah commanded it, she did as she was told. She did not happily go into this marriage. She saw the betrothal as a limitation of her power and her influence was starting to grow, which is one of the reasons Sarah insisted on the marriage. Rebekah had to be put into her proper place. It was as if Sarah could let the growth go so far but then had to limit it, and felt like the marriage would limit it perfectly; allowing her still to have influence and importance, respect, but not to go too far. There was a concern within Sarah that Rebekah would go too far, and she had to be limited, reined in.

Rebekah did agree to it and there was a camaraderie. Isaac, because he was of such a strong mother, could handle a strong wife. It is why they were well-matched in Sarah's eyes and Sarah was correct. They were strong personalities, but they balanced each other beautifully, not to the same degree that Sarah balanced Abraham, but in a similar way. Isaac was not Abraham. Isaac had his weaknesses. Isaac had more fears, and his faith sometimes was weaker. Rebekah helped him nurture his faith. Rebekah had the strength of faith that Isaac did not have and so it was a good matching, but it did take an ordering for her (Rebekah) to allow it.

#3 Recording 57:54 Finding Isaac a Wife

DR: In the Bible, the story was that a servant was sent by Abraham to go to a relative and find a wife for Isaac. So, Rebekah was living at some distance?

DS: No. We see Rebekah at Sarah's wing. We see Rebekah present to where they all are, but Rebekah was not of Abraham or Sarah. She was of Sarah's family, but she had been brought to Sarah at a young age when her wit and her intelligence was recognized. And so, she had come from a distance, but she had not been distanced at the time of being betrothed, no.

#3 *Recording 58:55 Rebekah's Deceiving Isaac with the Blessing for Jacob*

DR: The story of Rebekah when Isaac was dying, she deceived Isaac into giving his blessing to the son Jacob and not to the older son Esau. That's the story in the Bible, that she deceived Isaac.

DS: Rebekah did covet power. It was why she was betrothed to Isaac, to limit it (her power). But within her mind there was still a coveting of power. She was able, through Isaac, to exercise some power and influence and she enjoyed that. And she was very aware at the death of Isaac, she could lose her place. It was a selfish act. It was important to her to maintain her influence and we are going to suggest that her actions were selfish in her nature. She wanted the son she had more influence with to be given the blessing. She loved her children with her whole heart, but she loved her influence a little more than she should have. Sarah saw it as sinful. As Rebekah grew in age she learned how to hide it, so that she was not thought to be sinful anymore. But come the death of Isaac, there was a fear in her of who she would no longer be. A fear in her of who she would be now. So, she sought blessing to the son that she had the most influence with, so that she could hold her position. And so, there is truth to the story. But in one son being more blessed than other, it simply bestowed on that blessed son more power, more inheritance, more respect. The other son was not rejected or harmed in any way. But much less powerful, much less influential.

#3 Recording 1:01:41 Death of Rebekah

DR: Where and how did Rebekah die and how old was she?

DS: Rebekah saw her grandchildren. Rebekah saw her grandchildren married and pregnant. But it does not feel like she saw her great-grandchildren.

Show me the ending of the life of this one called Rebekah. Show me now please.

Rebekah took risks after Isaac passed. She was intrusive with her son who was blessed. She was intrusive in his life. So, she was not well-liked or well respected by the wives of her sons, the blessed one nor the other. That, in turn, lost some of her influence.

Her selfish need for influence grew stronger and embittered her. It caused her to take risks. We tell you this because it does not feel to us that her death was natural. It feels accidental. It feels as if she was in some place she should not have been. Feels as if she put herself in the path of her own death. I cannot see the circumstances, but she was someplace she shouldn't have been.

She would not be told the dangers, where she was. She would not hear such an order. The very warning that was given to her was what caused her death. I cannot see what it was. She died quickly. It feels as if something hit on her head, and she dies instantly. She was definitely in a place she should not have been.

Unfortunately for her, there was relief at her death in her family, because she had become difficult and demanding. So, her death was not an easy one. When she passed, she (her spirit) stayed with her family, with her body, because it was only through her passing that she saw her error. There was like another ceremony between her and her God, and there was forgiveness for she recognized her error, her sin, selfish pride, influence. There was fear in her at her passing that she would be punished for this. She found, experienced, **a compassion from the God she knew and no punishment.** As if her realization was punishment enough, that called her to stay around, to try to breach the prayer spaces of some of the other women, to try to teach about selfish pride, selfish need for influence and compassion of God. **For she did not know of compassion of God until after her passing, and she experienced that compassion.** So likewise, there was an eagerness for her to incarnate again so she could bring teachings of the compassion. But again, there was a sense of having to wait until the appropriate time.

It is interesting to us because we cannot see any influence of The Counsel here. We can feel an influence, of something that was orchestrating the timing of the teachings. For the teachings that she would bring on a compassionate God could not be brought until a certain point in the journey of evolution. So, all I can say is that feels like it is Creation or Creator, but I cannot be certain of that which I witness except there was **an orchestrated decision between her soul and her god of when she would bring these compassionate teachings.**

In this last section, after the death of Rebekah, Donna is now following the journey of the soul of Rebekah after her death. She can follow her journey beyond life. Within that following, Donna perceives the orchestration and decision about the death moment realization of Rebekah and how her soul then chooses to bring these understandings back to the Earth in another lifetime. That being said, Donna is also perceiving, that at this point, the orchestration of when these teachings can be brought to the Earth has nothing to do with The Counsel but perhaps of Creation/Creator itself. She cannot be sure, but Donna could feel a power orchestrating and working with the soul of Rebekah.

#3 Recording 57:01 *Rebekah's Contributions to the Tribe*

DR: Can you tell us what Rebekah contributed?

DS: Rebekah struggled. She was afraid to explore how intelligent she was. She didn't want to be smarter than her husband. There was a shyness in her that sometimes made it hard for her to be forward or outspoken. But there was a kindness in her, a softness in her. We want to say that people told her things; she was a confidante. She did not do this in manipulation. It was natural for her to listen; she was a natural listener. And because she was a natural listener, she had access to information that her husband would not have had access to. And so, her influence came more from what she heard in her listening and then retold to her husband that proved to be useful in different situations. She was not a spy or manipulator. She was a kind listener, but everything she heard she presented to her husband. There were no secrets between her and her husband. She was not a secret confidante and people knew that what you said to Rebekah, you said to her husband. But sometimes they could tell Rebekah when they could not tell any male, and so often Rebekah brought to the surface things that needed to be known, needed to be addressed.

Discussion

REBEKAH

Rebekah's Sin and Redemption

DS: When Rebekah, I want to say, once away from Sarah's influence, did not become a nice woman, and more so after the death of Isaac, because of doing her selfish thing, it was like that sin weighed on her soul. And so, it affected her that she had done this to her sons, and so she didn't become a nice person. She went further into her selfishness, further into her pridefulness of influence, and became more demanding, became more intrusive, wouldn't be told, wouldn't be put in her place. I couldn't see her death, but it was like she went somewhere she shouldn't have been, because it was dangerous and sure enough it was dangerous. And when she passed, there was relief in the family because she had become difficult in the family. She had become a difficult presence. But what was really interesting to see was her die expecting to be judged, because in her passing she recognized what she had been, what she had become. She expected to be judged and punished for it, and she wasn't! (*said with amazement*). And this was astounding to her that she was not brought to task and punished by God, but that there was a compassion offered to her.

That changed something. I want to say, it is at a soul level that made her want to come back immediately, so that people would know that there was compassion and love in God. And again, there was like a hold put on that. As if, and I don't believe this is possible personally, but as if the soul is not allowed to choose when it is coming back, but it was going to come back in a very specified time. It felt deliberate to me, but I could not identify delivered from where or delivered from whom or delivered from what, but there was a deliberateness in the evolution of the faith, of the belief systems. It was quite interesting.

Chapter Seven

RACHEL

So Isaac sent for Jacob and blessed him... "You shalt not take a wife from among the Canaanite women. Up, go to Paddan-aram, to the house of Bethuel, your mother's father, and take a wife there from among the daughters of Laban, your mother's brother". (Genesis 28:1-2)

Rachel came with her father's flock for she was a sheperdess. And when Jacob saw Rachel, the daughter of his uncle Laban, and the flock of his uncle Laban, Jacob went up and rolled the stone of the mouth of the well, and watered the flock of his uncle Laban. Then Jacob kissed Rachel, and broke into tears. (Genesis 29:9-11)

Jacob did so, he waited out the bridal week of the one, and then he (Laban) gave him his daughter as wife. (Genesis 29:28)

#3 Recording 24:31 *Story of Rachel*

DR: I want to ask about the third Matriarch, Rachel.

DS: Do you know her lineage, Rachel of...

DR: I think she was a cousin related to the Abraham family and the story is Jacob, the son of Rebekah, went to meet her to find a wife.

DS: We have the appropriate Rachel, one moment please.

A kind one with deep inner strength, willfulness, some pride, tried to be holy and it did not fit well upon her. There was too much intelligence and too much will. She was a student of the ways of Sarah, we would not say she was a student of Sarah, but she was a student of the ways of Sarah; power, decisive, clear supportive of those that were in her family. She did not bow easily to sacrifice or penance, and she did not like the feeling of being wrong or of sin. She disputed definitions of sin and sinfulness.

Rachel had her own ideas. She disagreed with the men in the circle of her life, and she did not hide her disagreement. She was able to obey, but not easily and not without words to say about what her obedience meant. She always needed to be clear, "I'm doing as you say but what you want to understand is this is why".

Rachel continued to teach as Sarah did for strength, decisiveness, awareness in the women. She did not for a moment believe that the God could only be heard by a select few. She did not hear God well in her prayers, but she sought to hear God as often as she could. She struggled with that listening, but she never gave up on hearing God's word. We will not say she heard it regularly, but she heard it often enough to encourage her to continue.

Feels to us as if she bore three children of the same father. They were her offerings to God: her body, her pregnancies, her children. These were offerings to God, not sacrifices. She did so willingly and with joy.

In the passage above, Donna has connected to the person Rachel was and so speaks descriptively about her. Donna can sense her beliefs, her strengths. She is sensing her from the inside out and so the description is personal and of the woman that Rachel was.

#3 Recording 24:35 Rachels' Meeting of Jacob

DR: How did she meet and marry Jacob?

DS: At first Jacob was, we don't want to say forced on her, but brought to her with little of her choice. Rachel did object; she didn't fight it, but she did object at first. But then she decided to listen to him and not the others. They had several meetings where it was as if she asked him many questions of his faith, of his relationship with God, of his ability to hear God. Others who knew of these conversations were quite affronted. She should have just done as she was told, to take the man that was willing to take her. But Jacob was not offended. He was intrigued. They came to strengthen each other's faith because they came together through these conversations.

It doesn't feel like it was love. It feels like it was respect and faith and honour. They mutually decided to agree to the marriage.

From the outside looking in, she was obeying. It was like an arranged marriage that she was accepting. But her and Jacob knew the truth of it... and one other. Another elder also knew. I'm not sure who it was, but an older man who sat with them during their conversations, because it would not have been right for her to be alone. He witnessed, without interference, their conversations, her questions, Jacob's answers, and understood what they were becoming to each other. This enabled her to support Jacob with completeness and enabled her to birth his sons and give them as gifts to Jacob, to the tribe, to God. So, Jacob's attentions in marriage were welcomed by Rachel and that allowed her to blossom because Jacob had the measure of her and understood her to be what could be his own Sarah. This made him feel very blessed and he looked at Rachel as a blessing that God was giving him, because she had many of the same expressions and thinking as Sarah.

DR: How old was Rachel when she married him and did she live far away and have to be brought in from a distance?

DS: She was from another tribe. *I don't know if that's the right word.* She came from a day's travel away and there was a question of the measure of that tribe. It feels as if it was quite a logical decision to bring in new blood and it was a bettering for Rachel, her family, and her tribe. As if there was a question of them being of a lesser class or caste. So, the travel she took to have these conversations with Jacob was frowned upon. She should have been happy with what they were offering her. But the elder who witnessed, and Jacob himself, encouraged it, and so there were three times she travelled to meet with Jacob. And it was the fourth travelling that created the marriage. That was the ceremony day.

#3 Recording 33:00 *Rachel, Related to the Tribe of Abraham*

DR: Was Rachel related to the Abraham clan?

DS: *Show me the family lines please. Show me now.*

The family line connects to Sarah's side but quite distant. We cannot even put a label to it. It was that distant. It was important. They wanted to bring new blood into the tribe. So, there was an understanding of Sarah and her teachings. There was an understanding that there was a link in the bloodline, but it was very, very distant, almost removed three times by marriage. But if we had to give her a family line connected to the Abraham-Sarah, we would say it is connected on the side of Sarah, quite distant.

#3 Recording 34:27 *Rachel Questioning Jacob about His Faith*

DR: When Rachel questioned Jacob about his beliefs, can you tell us examples of the kinds of questions or content of some of those questions, just a few examples?

DS: Questions she asked would be an affront to a man, but she asked them anyway. The elder was shocked to witness, but Jacob stopped him and answered questions such as how often he prayed; what did he see and felt when he prayed; did he believe he could hear God; did he believe she could hear God.

It was more about his faith and then to be sure his faith was demonstrated in his behaviour. She asked for an example of something he did to honour his God through his own decisions, an honourable action he took for his God in alignment to his beliefs. Her concern was that his beliefs and his behaviours were strongly tied.

#3 Recording 36:03 Rachel's Relationship with Rebekah and Sarah

DR: What was Rachel's relationship with her mother-in-law Rebekah and Sarah, because Sarah was still alive?

DS: She worships Sarah. Sarah was uncomfortable with that and encouraged Rachel to be in her own power and her own relationship with God, not to try and copy. But Rachel still emulated. With Rebekah there was challenge. Rebekah also knew of the teachings of Sarah, but did not have the strength of character, will, to be as willful as Rachel and Sarah were. Rebekah did sometimes frown upon the willfulness of Rachel. But Jacob was always the supporter of Rachel and so Rebekah was silenced by Jacob, because of Rebekah's respect for men, for Jacob's word, in Jacob's marriage.

Rebekah did not have the influence with Rachel that a mother-in-law would have expected, and she was insulted by this at times. But it feels like she had no one to turn to because there were more women who followed the teachings of Sarah than the teachings of the old ways of servitude. Rebekah had more servitude in her. She was willful and intelligent and supported her husband as best she could, the way Sarah taught. But she was not as good at it. She was not strong enough in her willfulness, strong enough in her character to stand as women like Rachel stood. Rebekah stood a little more timid, a little more subservient. But she did not like Rachel and her ways.

#3 Recording 38:12 *Rachel Conceiving Children*

DR: Was Rachel barren?

DS: I want to say no. I see two sons and one daughter, and so I would say no.

#3 Recording 38:46 *Rachel Giving Her Maidservants to Jacob to Have Children*

DR: The story of Rachel giving her maidservants to Jacob to conceive children, the same as the story of Abraham, can you tell me about that story?

In this next section, Donna speaks about perceiving an "anger" in the response. In Donna's connection in channel to this information, she is also aware of emotional responsiveness as well as words. It is interesting that at this idea of maidservants being "given" to create children I expressed, there is anger and insult at such a question. Donna cannot say who or where this is coming from specifically. It is more that, as she opens for the words to answer this question, she is met first with anger and insultedness. As well, as Donna communicates in words the answer, she can also feel a sense of being compelled to speak with the disgust that she can feel. This is not disgust or anger from Donna. It is coming from wherever these words are coming from. Most interesting.

DS: I do not know where this is coming from but this second question again about maidservants and the children raises an angry response. I perceive an angry response, that insulted response. It feels like these stories were made to dispute, wrong word, to disrespect women of great strength and great faithfulness.

I cannot see anything but monogamy in these marriages. What we want to say to you is this is behaviour of the unfaithful. It is the unfaithful that have children with their servants. It is not the faithful who do this. *There is disgust and anger at the question.*

I cannot identify where this response is coming from.

We are adamant in expressing it to you that is only those of the unfaithful that would have children with their servants. This is not the behaviour of the faithful. The stories of such were made to bring into dispute the faithfulness of those that were faithful, to tarnish image and respect. We would suggest to you that the stories were made by the <u>unfaithful men who did have children with their servants</u> and wanted those of the higher echelon of the tribe to have the same behaviour, so they would not be shamed. They were to be shamed. This did not happen. It was not condoned.

#3 *Recording 41:08* <u>*Rachel's Children*</u>

DR: So, if Jacob had three children with Rachel, did he have other children (not mentioned above)?

DS: *Show me Rachel's pregnancy line, show me now please.*

There were three children with Rachel and then there was a pause. Feels like Rachel was unwell perhaps as long as a year or two. Then there were more children with Rachel, but she became unwell again. After her death Jacob had more children with a second wife, but only after Rachel had passed. So, there are multiple children to Jacob, first with Rachel and then with another woman.

DR: But only three children with Rachel?

DS: No. Rachel had three children and then there was a pause, because she was unwell. So, then there would be two years with no children and then more children with Rachel.

DR: (Do) you see how many more?

DS: *Show me the timeline please.* One child, male. Two children, twins, one female, one male. Two more males. One more female. She was unwell with the last child and her death occurred either in childbirth or very soon after.

It was a great loss to Jacob. The second wife became a duty. Also, before Rachel left, she made him promise that he would not remain alone, that he needed the support of a good woman and the support of more family. So out of duty he married again.

#3 *Recording 48:48 Children by Jacob's Second Wife*

DR: So, when he married again how many more children were there?

DS: This woman was younger, filled with vitality, ten or twelve maybe more. At least 10.

DR: 10 more children?

DS: Yes.

#3 *Recording 44:17 Rachel Stealing Idols*

DR: The story of Rachel, in her early years, of stealing two idols from the relative named Laban, L-a-b-a-n. Tell us about this story of her stealing two idols.

DS: She did not steal them; she removed them.

One moment please. Creator, may we know who this voice is that I am hearing, this one of anger and outrage? May we know who this is please? If it is to be spoken show me now.

I cannot put a name to this voice I sense. It feels like one who is very faithful. It is one who supported, would almost feel like a saint if we used your human terminology. It feels like a saint who supported these tribes connected to Abraham. One who answered the prayers on behalf of the God and supported them like a saint or an angel. It is not an angel, more like a saint.

And again, when you ask of these idols, there's an anger in this one.

She did not steal. She removed idols from where they did not belong. She felt she was being faithful to her beliefs and to the beliefs of the tribe. That the idols she removed, should not have been where they were. They were not stolen. Do you understand?

DR: Yes. Did she destroy them or just hide them?

DS: She gave them to the poorest and simplest of that area. Not of their tribe, but of that area so they could be sold and help those who were the poorest. She suffered for it. The one she took them from did strap her, and she did not cry out. I want to say she did not bleed, as if there was something miraculous, because she was doing God's work in removing those idols. She was punished, but was righteous in her punishment, strong in her punishment. It was the beginning of her strength.

DR: She was strapped; she was whipped?

DS: Yes, because it was perceived to be stolen. She removed that which did not belong, in a place that it should not be. It was sacrilegious and she was making it right. She was young; she was impetuous; she was disrespectful; but her heart was clear.

#3 Recording 58:53 Rachel's Contributions to the Tribe

DR: What did Rachel contribute?

DS: Rachel understood things differently; she understood the dynamics. She was not a listener. She was one who figured, one who looked at the dynamics and looked for another way, another solution, another approach, and so she brought a different viewpoint. Always to her husband, no one else. But she helped sometimes to see things from a different angle. Rachel had a sight that took a different view. As well, in her prayer space, she could see dynamics interplaying between people of the tribe and she could see where someone would be better served or where their skill could be better used. So, there was an insight that she achieved in her prayer space as well. So, it was her insight, her ability to see other perspectives, other uses for skills, other uses for people, other uses for resources.

#5 Recording 4:33 Rachel and the Idols

DR: The question is about Rachel, who took some idols. Who did she take these idols from and why do they not belong where they were, as she felt.

DS: Can we have more of an identification of which Rachel we are tuning into please?

DR: This is the third Matriarch, Rachel, who married Jacob the son of Isaac.

DS: There is strength in this one, determination, and willfulness. She is clear in her thinking and she is clear in her beliefs and that her beliefs are the beliefs. She believes she is aligned to the teachings. Your question again please about the idols.

DR: Yes, who did she take the idols from and why does she think the idols didn't belong where they were?

DS: It feels to us that this one had discussions with others concerning these idols. This was not a snap decision. She spoke to her husband. She spoke to the other women of wisdom, and she prayed with this. She felt there was a meaning coming with these idols, that the symbolism of the idols was becoming stronger than she felt it should.

We will say that the others she spoke to did not see a problem forming the way she did. She perceived this to be the start of something that needed to be stopped immediately, that needed to be nipped in the bud, not allowed to develop at all. But there was no disagreement with her, so much as there was a neutrality with those she spoke to as if they thought she was making something bigger of this than it was. This is what caused her to take it on for herself and to make a decision, to take an action.

As we've said in the opening, we can feel her certainty in her faith, her certainty in the beliefs. There was an aspect of herself that was guarding the beliefs with this action. She was proactive in that way. But for some she was too picky, too expectant. Some felt that her measuring stick was harsher than it needed to be.

We move more deeply into this event, one moment please.

It feels like it was a few weeks in decision before she took this action. There were several reasons why it was taken. First, was that those who had the idols were richer and not, in her opinion, sharing their wealth well. That the idols were representative of their wealth, not of what they meant to represent. Rachel supported equality in the tribe and did not feel this was appropriate for a single family or a single line to hold these idols.

She did not consider the action stealing and there was some concern in the discussion she had with others that this could be perceived as stealing. But she had no intention of keeping them. She was taking them to be put in a place where they were in a more appropriate place, where they could be appreciated or enjoyed by all, the true symbolism of it could be recognized.

Rachel did not sneak in and steal. She went in daylight, commanded attention, and she took these with the knowledge of those who owned them.

There was a lecture given, words spoken by her to explain her actions and she would not take no for an answer. She told them she was taking them. She told them where she was taking them to and why she was taking them and then stalked off. It does not feel like there were dozens. It feels like there was enough that she could carry. She took them to a place of worship or place of community so that they would be the property of all, appreciated by all.

She made a show of where she placed them, wherever this was, so that anyone passing by would know that she had put them here deliberately and that they were here now for all to appreciate, enjoy, and use.

There was a sense of use to them as if they could create a point of focus. Once they were placed, it feels to us as if she stomped off, achieved her purpose, and moved into the rest of her day. Rachel did not care about chastisement or retrieval. She felt that she had done this so publicly that retrieval could not just be them being taken back, but would have to be brought into discussion. Wherever she put them, whether it was a community or a center or temple, wherever she put them they could not just be taken back. They needed to be discussed, because she put them there vocally and with reason, and so the reasons would have to be answered before the owner could take them back. So, she had established what she wanted to establish, and then moved off into her day.

There was disagreement, not of what she had done, but how she had done it, and there was quite a bit of agreement in what she had done. There was some who saw this as stealing but not many. Those that were in disagreement, it was more that she was attributing more value, *wrong word*, more disruption to these idols than they were worth; that they did not signify what she was afraid they were signifying. They did not signify wealth. They did not signify inequality. They did not signify worship. There were those who disagreed with her and those were the terms of the disagreement. It was never about the taking. It was why she took that there was disagreement. There was also quite a few that agreed, and did not see the need, even where she placed them, did not see the need for them to be there at all.

There was some defending of these idols. That they had been made in the love of God, that they have been made symbolic, but Rachel did not feel that that is how they were being used. And that was the concern, that this was degrading the prayer, the connection, that the idols were unnecessary. If they were made in the love of God, then they must be kept where all could use them and not just one family or one line.

It feels like that disagreement continued. It doesn't feel like her moving the idols was the end of it. It feels like it created discussions for weeks among the wise men, among the men of the tribe and among the women of the tribe. She was pleased with this, for that is what she wanted. She wanted this to be discussed. She wanted this to be in the eyes of all. This be what we see around this. Further questions of this matter?

DR: So were these idols of gods, like the Canaanite gods?

DS: They were artistic representations to demonstrate the love that artists had for, *I can't use the word gods*, for miracle, for sanctuary. There was gratitude in them as the artist would defend. But they had somehow become more than that. They had lost their true symbolism and became a focal point, a demonstration of wealth, a demonstration of artistry. The beginnings, Rachel's fear was, of inequality. They also became focal points for prayer, for meditation, and again her fear was that the ability to pray, to meditate without focal point could be lost. Rachel did not agree with the need of them. It feels to us as if these were created in gratitude, appreciation, and love for what they represented but the owners did not seem to hold them that way.

The owners were not the artists. The owners had paid for them from the artist. As we said there was discussion around this. The artists were questioned. The artists did this out of gratitude, out of love, trying to depict the miraculous, trying to depict that which there was not a vision of. That was acceptable except when the artist sold these idols they became possessions, they became demonstrations of wealth. There was a fear in Rachel that they would become something worse than that.

DR: So, these did not belong to her family or her father.

DS: The house she took them from she had access to. She would not have been stopped from entering. *Is this the house of her father?*

It does not feel like the house of her father. If this had been in the house as a father, she would have done this differently. There would have been more emotion, a different level of concern. This feels like an important person in the tribe, in the area, but still accessible to her. Someone that would not easily be questioned. Perhaps one of the wise men or one of the elders, teachers. Someone that people did not question and yet she had been watching and questioned. Part of the effect of what she did was that she questioned someone who would not be questioned by most and caused this one to defend their ownership of these idols, which was the whole point of the exercise. So, Rachel achieved exactly what she wanted to achieve, and it did come to a point where it did not matter now what happened to the idols because the issue, the concern she had, had been raised by her actions. So, we would say no, this was not her father.

Discussion

RACHEL

Rachel Questioning Jacob, Untruth of Offering Handmaidens to Husbands

DR: So I was really, really thrilled that you could get the answers to the questions that Rachel asked Jacob in three sessions. This happened temporally, this happened three and a half thousand years ago, plus or minus. And the questions are still there, and then the anger over the handmaidens being given to, the anger is still there. It didn't dissipate over time.

DS: I could see Rachel sitting with Jacob and I could see a very old man, white-haired, white beard, quite stout, sitting there as the chaperone. And Rachel asking her questions of Jacob and the old man wanting to stop her, "How dare you!" and Jacob just raised his hand and said, "Leave her". And he answered her questions. He wanted her questions because he was also taking the measure of her, and he stopped the elder from stopping Rachel, because Rachel would have been stopped.

DR: You don't know if that was his father, Isaac?

DS: I don't think so. I don't think so, but it was a very old man with a white, white beard, long white hair, quite stout, very authoritarian. It could have been a father. It could have been some type of a minister or priest, a holy man of some type, but he was there as the chaperone. He was there to keep Rachel in line, not Jacob. But Jacob wouldn't let that happen. He wanted to know the measure and so he welcomed her questions. They had that; that was the start of their partnership, was them exploring, you know, him seeing; Jacob seeing what kind of a partner she would be. I could see the two of them sitting there and Jacob not intimidated by her questions; Jacob welcoming her questions and answering them with all honesty. She wanted him to prove that he was the man of his faith, that his prayers made him look like he was, "Prove to me you are a man of faith. Prove to me that you've made decisions in alignment to God, that you've done the difficult things. Prove this to me". The elder was just outraged that she would ask such a thing. "How dare you make him prove himself?" But Jacob, I could literally see him put a hand up like this and go (Donna motions) and just answered her. It was a remarkable experience because they were two extremely faithful people discussing how they walked their faith. She wanted to know how he walked his faith, you know. It was fascinating.

I can't help but feel that came from Sarah. I'd love to have lunch with her, boy, that's cool. But the anger, outrage, that's still there, to use your words. I like that; it is still there. It's like someone witnessed the stories being made from another, from the other plane, from, I don't know, heaven, from being dead and was outraged at such a thing being written. It really felt like that whole story was created so that the men that wanted otherwise, to the women that had children with servants, there is nothing wrong with that; it was done before; it's always been done. **But it's not the truth.** It's not the truth, because that's not a partnership that's not a respectful partnership between a man and a woman. As I perceived it, that marriage then was a respectful partnership. It was not a servitude; you weren't owned. No, there was no ownership. Fascinating, what fun this is!

Chapter Eight

LEAH

Now Laban had two daughters; the name of the older one was Leah, and the name of the younger one was Rachel. Leah had weak eyes. Rachel was shapely and beautiful. Jacob loved Rachel; so he answered, "I will serve you seven years for your daughter Rachel." (Genesis 29:16-18)

#3 Recording 42:35 The Story of Leah

DR: So, switching to Leah. Leah was also married, in the story, to Jacob. The story of Jacob was that he was working to obtain Rachel as a wife, and then was given Leah instead of Rachel, and had to work longer to get Rachel. So, the story of Leah?

DS: *Show me Rachel; show me Jacob; show me Leah; show me now please.*

It feels to us that Leah was in love with Jacob. That Leah wanted Jacob. It was before Rachel, but she was not the woman for Jacob. She was not strong enough. Leah was not wise enough; she was too adoring. *Ah, here is the reason for the story.* Sarah would not approve of Leah as a wife of Jacob. Leah was not strong enough yet for... *why?* Leah did not know her own power yet. She was too subservient, too adoring. Sarah was the one who said no to Leah and helped to find someone outside, of a different bloodline, that was strong enough for Jacob.

DR: So, they were not sisters, Leah and Rachel?

DS: No. It feels to us as if Leah was of the same tribe as Sarah, and Rachel was of a tribe distant, distant, distant related, but a day's travel away.

DR: So, Leah was never a wife of Jacob? She did not have children with him?

DS: No. She wanted such and was vindictive when Sarah refused her.

DR: She lived in the same vicinity as Abraham, as Rebekah and the family?

DS: Yes, and did her best to dispute the integrity and honour of Rachel. She married and had children but always adoring Jacob.

#3 Recording 50:33 *Leah's Children*

DR: How many children did she have?

DS: We want to say she was competitive with Rachel. She wanted to be thought of as a better wife than Rachel. So, she tried at every turn to have more children than Rachel, to do everything better than Rachel.

Can I see the pregnancy line please?

She had more children than Rachel because in the two years that Rachel was unwell, she (Leah) had children. So, we would say she had two or three children more than Rachel.

#3 Recording 51:31 Leah Having Weak Eyes

DR: The story of Leah having weak eyes and also of being not pretty, the intent was to say she was not pretty, where did this come from?

DS: Weak eyes was a saying used, a euphemism for her lack of wisdom, that she did not see the truth. She saw what she wanted to see. She saw what mattered to her. She saw love in Jacob when there was no love. She saw jealousy in Rachel, when there was no jealousy. She saw anger in Sarah where there was no anger. So, the euphemism of weak of eyes was seeing not with truth, seeing what she wanted to see. Those who would say she was not pretty would not speak of her skin, they spoke of her spirit, her jealousy, her pettiness, her competitiveness, her anger and disappointment.

#3 Recording 52:51 Leah's Role in the Hebrew Bible

DR: So why does she have a big role in the Hebrew Bible?

DS: There is a need, as the Bible was composed, to weaken the role of women, to weaken the teachings of Sarah. So, some of the women that were not supportive of the Sarah teachings or did not walk the Sarah teachings as well as others, were made more of and those that walk the teachings of Sarah were made less than. So, there is a lack of equality among how the women are displayed and those who are of power are displayed as less than. Those who are more subservient, are more what women were supposed to be, those women of lesser character became more in the stories.

DR: So, then Leah had no real effect, impact, on the Hebrews or her lineage, had no other impact upon the Hebrews?

DS: The answer to your question about Leah specifically, is that it is because of who she married. As if she married into a line of importance. She did so again to compete with Rachel, to see that her husband was more than Jacob, worth more than Jacob. So, because of that lineage she was included in the stories.

Discussion

LEAH

#3 Recording 1:08:27 *Matriarchs*

Marriages Not Romantic, but Arranged. Leah Not a Good Match for Jacob.

DS: Marriages were not romantic. They were partnered and women were chosen deliberately. That's why the first woman who was in love with Jacob, Leah, she was adoring of Jacob, she was in love with Jacob, and Sarah knew this would not make a good partner. She would not partner Jacob; she would tell Jacob what he wanted to hear. She would, no, she had to be able to stand equal to Jacob. Marriages were partners and Sarah supported that. Then, that left a bitter anger, left a bitterness in Leah. So that created, you know, competition with Rachel. She was gossipy and bad-mouthing to her.

Section Three

OTHER BIBLICAL WOMEN OF NOTE

Chapter Nine

DINAH

Now Dinah, the daughter that Leah had borne to Jacob, went out to visit the daughters of the land, Shechem, son of Hamor the Hivite, chief of the country, saw her, and took her and lay with her by force. Being strongly drawn to Dinah, daughter of Jacob, and in love with the maiden, he spoke to the maiden tenderly. So Shechem said to his father Hamor, "Get me this girl as a wife." (Genesis 34:1-4)

#5 Recording 19:39 *Other Women*

The Story of Dinah

DR: So, moving on, the story of Dinah, D-i-n-a-h, who was supposed to be violated by a non-Hebrew, Shechem, and the Hebrews slaughtered men of that other tribe.

DS: Spell the name again for me please?

DR: Dinah, D-i-n-a-h.

DS: Youthful, innocent, a bit naive, very trusting, younger than her years, but there was strength in her. She was not a fool. She was practical and grounded. She would have been described as a good daughter to her mother. She was obedient, but occasionally in demonstrating the strength of her will, she did disobey. There were desires to know more, to be more within her, some would have said "above her station." But it wasn't above her station; it was that there was an intellect within her that wanted to be more educated, wanted to understand, and that is where she danced a bit with obedience. She did not want to obey without understanding. Now your question specific to this one please.

DR: The Bible story says she was involved with or violated by a man from outside the tribes who actually wanted to marry her, but then the Hebrew men of her tribe retaliated, slew a lot of the other men outside of the tribe.

DS: As we perceive this person you speak of it feels to us as if this is more about education. There were things she wanted to learn that the men within the tribe would not teach her, and the women within the tribe did not know. She went to this man to learn and, what has been called violations, he taught her. He expanded her mind; he taught her things that women were not taught. He allowed her to question things that women did not question. He allowed her to step outside the tribe and the faith, and question things. The violation in your story is that violation. That her very feminine self was violated in the intellect, in the mind. We do see retaliation. It does not feel like it was quite as severe as your story says. This man was punished physically; his family was punished, and others close to him were punished. It did result in an ostracize as if there was some sharing of supplies or some sharing of product that this one was now barred from the tribal village to offer his wares. He was a teacher and he now would no longer be a teacher connected to the tribe, no longer teach the boys.

It feels like he violated the trust of the tribe by teaching her. It does not feel like it was a physical violation and we do not see romance here; we see learning. What was most terrible, and we would suggest how your story came to be, was that what she had learned she could not unlearn; what she had heard she could not un-hear, once she had questioned, she could not stop questioning. So, when she returned to the tribe, she disturbed the waters. She brought questions to the other women, questions to her family and the men in her family. It took a long time for that to calm, for her to find balance again, acceptance again.

It does not feel like it created a war between tribes but it did sever relationships. So, if there were supplies coming from his tribe, they were no longer allowed into this tribe. This one was a teacher and this one you have named, Dinah, was one who needed to learn. The questions she brought back, first to the women and then to her family of origin, her father, her mother, disturbed the waters, but also opened up minds in new directions. It did create quite a wave, a ripple effect that lasted a few years, because some of her questions could not be answered through faith.

So, it disturbed the faithful, it disturbed the status quo, and it created a ripple effect that also ignited other questionings. Minds started to question things they did not question before. Not everyone, not all the time, not all at once, but it seeded the idea of airing the question and this disturbed the balance and the status quo greatly. So, it was viewed as a violation, and it took many years to heal that violation, to find the strength of the status quo again, to re-establish it. And it was never really re-established. There were questions asked quietly, discussions had quietly. Not often, but with some regularity two or three times a year, things that would not have been questioned were questioned and discussed, and solace was found; answer was found. It was a good thing, but it was not perceived to be so by those who wanted the status quo maintained.

#5 Recording 26:46 *Other Women*

Teacher of Dinah

DR: This teacher, was he of a different Hebrew tribe or not of the Hebrews?

DS: He was of a different Hebrew tribe, and it was the fact that he allowed the questions and discussed the questions and sought answers to the questions that was the violation.

#5 Recording 27:16 *Other Women*

What Did Dinah Want to Learn?

DR: What did she want to learn, and what did she learn from him?

DS: The question asked most often was why. Why certain rules, certain habits, certain methods? Why were certain behaviours expected of men, of women?

She was perceived to be petulant or disobedient when she did this in her own home. Once he allowed her questions, would discuss her questions, she became silent in her home. Those in her home thought she had come to be obedient, had come around, but because she had a place where she could explore, she became quiet of questions elsewhere.

Show me the questions with more detail please show me now.

She questioned more often new rules, new ideas, *not new ideas*, **new rules** as if some of the older rules had been rewritten and strengthened. She wanted to know why. Why would the old rules be made stronger? Why would the old rules be changed at all? She did not question the oldest rule. She questioned the rewriting, the strengthening of those rules. She questioned how the old rules were being rewritten to seemingly limit and control women more than men, but still men as well. And this teacher responded because some of the questions she voiced, he had had in his heart, but did not have the courage to voice them. When Dinah voiced them, they could discuss, as if they were trying to take apart some of the new rules and find the original rule; find the original rule and the reason for the original rule, its purpose. For when they found the purpose of the original rule, they could attend that original rule; but they could not find the same purpose in these rules where the old ones were just strengthened or made more limiting or made more excluding. Some of the rules have been rewritten, because there was this sense of growth and expansion within the females, more than the males, but sometimes also within the younger boys. The elders were wanting to strengthen the rules to keep things in the status quo. There was a feeling that some of the new generation needed more stringent rules, more limitations, that the faith was not strong enough, and so the rules needed to be stronger. **It feels to us, as we witnessed it, that the rules were meant to strengthen the faith, but they did not have that result.** The questions of faith needed to be discussed as faith, but instead the answer to the question of faith became rules.

#5 Recording 31:06 Other Women

What Became of Dinah?

DR: What became of Dinah in the tribe, marriage, family, her faith, her role?

DS: She was not allowed to marry nor was she allowed to have children. Again, there was this thought that if they limited her, they could limit what she was spreading. They did not want her children to have her mind. It does not feel like she was married. It feels as if she attended her parents until their death and then attended the tribe like a maid, that's not the right word, but she attended the needs of the tribe. She was working off a penance in this. There was discussion. It wasn't one person's decision, but her questions seeded unrest, and it was as if the question had to be put down. So, she had to be put down.

Her movements were restricted; her knowledge was restricted; her access was restricted, and it was a sense of her in penance for the sin of questioning faith. **But she did not question faith**; she questioned rules. But it was perceived as the question of faith and so it was like she, *perhaps this is too strong to say*, but it was like she became a non-entity. She did die not long after her parents. She did not live a long life.

The loneliness, the restriction, the sense of sin weighed heavy on her. What started out in youthful exuberance, eagerness to understand the faith, had become quite destroyed. She did not take her own life, but she did not live long after the purpose of looking after her parents was done. She did not have enough purpose. We would almost say she died for lack of purpose, and her death was a relief to the elders. But there was always the seed of question from that one onwards, and we're suggesting that the story as written was to remember that such questioning was violation of the faith. **She did not question the faith. She questioned the men who ruled the faith**, and that was her error.

#5 Recording 34:01 Other Women

Whose Daughter Was Dinah?

DR: So, whose daughter was she, because the Bible says she was the daughter of Jacob and Leah.

DS: No…we would suggest she is the daughter of a cousin of Jacob, male cousin, father's side, about the same age as Jacob or slightly younger, but not of Jacob. No.

Discussion

DINAH

Control by Elders

DR: The other theme that's really emerging is one of control.

If you remember back to the very first session, book one, when I asked about the Matriarchs and their role: the men were trying to control this new endeavour and the women were trying to get them to let go of that control. Then all throughout, we see these indications of the men trying to control the process and then control the woman's knowledge, what they were able to learn. The story of Dinah…Dinah appears once in the Bible. So, this guy wanted to marry her and then they had relations, and then a horrible thing happened, slaughter. But again, it was a concocted story to cover up that this woman wanted to learn.

DS: Yes, and they also wanted to make it extremely dangerous to learn, like she was violated. She was punished. There was great death as a result of it. They were really, as I perceive it, strengthening the stories and the gruesomeness of the punishments for the things that they wanted to stop happening.

DR: Well, the Bible story says that the Hebrews made this, and it was an outside tribe, not Hebrews, made all these grown men get circumcised, and then they slaughtered them all.

I mean that's horrible! That's the Bible story. That's why people say the Bible has horrible things in it. Well yes, because it didn't happen.

DS: Also, because they were trying to control something that was uncontrollable. It was evolution; evolution is what it was. Of course, we wouldn't have known that.

#5 Recording 1:17:38 *Other Women*

Dinah Became the Excuse to Limit Women

DR: Dinah could have been a very helpful woman to the tribes, in the same way as the Matriarchs and others. She had the questioning ability. "Why do you do this? And if there is not a good reason, let's do something else". But her power was completely stripped.

DS: The other reason Dinah is included in the stories is because with what Dinah did that eroded the sum of the power that the women had achieved, because she went outside the tribe and asked questions and was taught. It was almost like the power and the education that Sarah had started had really gained a little bit of momentum. The story of Dinah, and I don't know what the timing is, because I don't know the Bible, but it felt to me like the story of Dinah gave the elders an excuse to start to pull back the power from women, to start to pull away the education of women. So, what Sarah had started, which was training women to be partners to husbands, that power was starting to be lost after Dinah. It's almost like Dinah started to ask questions in directions that they couldn't control, so they needed to then control the women and their learning, period. So, it's almost like Dinah symbolized the change, and that's why it was such a horrific story, because Dinah symbolized that point where the women went too far, and so they had to be corralled and brought right back in.

DR: So, this was early on, at least as far as the Bible story, because she was the daughter of one of the Matriarchs. In fact, they said Leah. But she was up there one generation below Jacob and Rachel, so this is quite early in the story.

DS: So, this is quite interesting, because I could feel, like I'm just putting it in what we talked about so I'm putting it out of order, but I could feel that when Dinah happened, it was the excuse they needed to limit women further. That's why she was called violated, because she was termed that, even though it wasn't a physical violation.

DR: So, this happened right after the three Matriarchs, you know, Sarah, Rebekah, and Rachel, who were very strong women in their own right. Then the next generation, what, got squashed then?

DS: Yes, exactly. So, is Dinah after Sarah?

DR: Well, according to the Bible, Dinah was after Rachel, the third Matriarch.

DS: Where is Sarah in that?

DR: Sarah is the first Matriarch.

DS: OK, from Sarah they started educating women differently to be partnered in equal with men. Dinah stopped that. Dinah was the finish of it. Dinah was the excuse they needed to stop it. That's why Dinah is in the Bible, because Dinah was a turning point, and they had to make sure that the stories told, the teachings told, limited it and showed it was dangerous, a violation. Because they couldn't control the mind.

Chapter Ten

MIRIAM

Then Miriam, the prophetess, Aaron's sister, took a timbrel in her hand, and all the women went out after her in dance with timbrels. (Exodus 15:20)

When they were in Hazeroth, Miriam and Aaron spoke against Moses because of the Cushite woman he had married: "He married a Cushite woman!" (Numbers 12:1)

The LORD came down in a pillar of cloud, stopped at the entrance of the Tent and called out, "Aaron and Miriam!" (Numbers 12:5).

As the cloud withdrew from the Tent, there was Miriam stricken with snow-white scales! (Numbers 12:10)

#6 Recording 5:09 Miriam

Story of Miriam

DR: My question is to explain the story of Miriam, who was the sister of Moses, her story, her role, her involvement, her impact.

Finding Her Strength and Identity

DS: *When we first connect to Miriam, she is in the background and then with our focus we bring her to the foreground.*

She feels very tied to her mother, taking from her mother all leadership in how to be. She feels younger than her years; it took a while for her child self to mature. She understood things at a young age and took them in, but how to portray them, how to be that, was a puzzle to her. She learned a lot by observation. She was aware of her brother and, regardless of her age, she feels younger and smaller than him. We do not mean that in stature.

There was some hesitancy within her, more when she was younger than older, but a hesitancy related to Moses. She felt like she needed to step back, was intimidated, not frightened exactly, but definitely intimidated. There was a strength in Moses even at a young age, and Miriam recognized that and was a little intimidated by it. She looked to her mother to understand what strength would look like for herself. She recognized the strength in Moses, but did not know if she was allowed to have strength, if she had strength, and so she would watch her mother, looking for strong moments. There were strong moments with mother. There was strength in the woman that was her mother. She recognized it and watched carefully to see how her mother managed that strength, spoke that strength, portrayed it.

There is a sense until about the early teens, perhaps twelve, that she was a bit portraying, like she did not completely understand herself or her role, and so she did as she was told; she acted like she thought everyone would expect her to be. Around the age of twelve something changed within her. It is like she saw herself differently, and started to know herself to be different from what she was told to do, different from what she was told to be. She had found her own strength, her own identity, but it's interesting to us that as she finds her own identity, there is this sense that she must hold it close, hide it. Miriam has watched her mother, and there's seemingly so many things her mother is that she does not demonstrate, that she does not portray to others. She would never call her mother secretive, and yet as Miriam finds this strength within herself, as she finds this sense of her own definition, she realizes what she saw in her mother that her mother did not show to others. So, Miriam again follows the same example.

#6 Recording 9:43 Miriam

Watching Moses' Faith

DS: From twelve until older Miriam had a different view of Moses as well. She watched him interestingly, saw his conflicts, saw his choices, saw his demonstration of bravery, saw his faith (*said quietly, with reverence*). The faith was curious to her, *that's not exactly the right word*. She witnessed and watched his faith and was curious. He seemed so calm within it. She likewise had faith, but she questioned it more.

Miriam did not have unquestionable faith, and so in her faith development she watched more often her brother than her mother. She watched how he walked with God. Her feeling inside is that her walk with God is more as a servant whereas Moses' walk with God was as equals, not the right word, but he was allowed to walk with God. For Miriam it felt more like she was to serve God. She never saw servitude in Moses, and it puzzled her. There is strong will within her as she develops, and her questions are deep and unspoken. There is obedience on her part, but it takes effort. She would, by others, be described as a good daughter. She would make a good wife, but the questions were within her.

As she grew and as Moses became all that he could be, she did find places with Moses to ask her questions. Moses was kind and patient. He did not treat her as a servant, but he did not like her questions. Better we would say he did not like her questioning, but he did his best to answer or discuss her questions. There were times he would chastise her for questions, and he would say that to question this was to question faith itself. *[Here seems to be a better explanation for Miriam being punished than the biblical Miriam questioning Moses' marriage (Numbers 12:1-15)]*

Miriam walked away from those conversations realizing she was not always sure what faith was, and that question of what faith was haunted her for most of her adult life. There were phases, times, where she was more certain in her faith. But sometimes, she did not know what Moses meant when he said she was questioning faith itself. She was the servant of God as she was told to be; she was the wife she was told to be; she was the daughter she was told to be. When she could be the servant of God, she understood her relationship better. But when she tried to explore the trust of God, the faith of God, there were questions here. She broached the subject once or twice with her mother, but could see the displeasure it caused. And so, the only one she discussed her questions of faith with was Moses, and even there she learned to be careful, because he would chastise her. When she questioned Moses about things, it sometimes puzzled him. Moses did not question God and so he did not understand why she would.

Miriam did not mean to question God. She just meant to question the way, the understandings, the necessities of the behaviour, of the acceptance. Miriam had a strong and good mind. Her heart was kind, but her heart was more in servitude as if she did not come from a place of loving kindness; she came from a place of duty-kindness. She was very dutiful, very faithful in her duties to family, husband, and friends. She knew her place in the tribe and was dutiful to it. We would say that very few people knew of her questions, very few people.

As she grew older, perhaps in her third decade into her fourth decade, she was a little more vocal, that's not the right word, a little more honest with her questions. She witnessed shifts in society, in the tribe. She witnessed growth in people's personalities, desires and wants, and that gave her reason, courage, bravery to speak her questions. She did not exactly expect answers. When she raised her questions, it was so others would think about what they did, think about what they demanded, think about what they expected. Miriam was never, her entire life, one of blind faith. She knew her God. She loved her God. But she could question her God, and it worried her sometimes that she was this way.

Her relationship with Moses grew a little more distant when there were other responsibilities for her. But always there was time Moses would give for her, perhaps not daily or even weekly, but there was time. It feels like Moses was more distant, unavailable to her. It is not like he travelled, but he wasn't present near her. He was elsewhere and so to spend time with him was a gift. It happened with some regularity, but more by happenstance. It was almost as if Moses remembered his sister and tried to give her time even if it was once a month or once every two or three months. There was a nurturing from Moses to his sister, but he was also, put very simply, a very busy man and there was a long period of time in his life where only those that were immediate to him were of his concern. He left his family, his mother, his sister, his parents to their part of the tribe, their part of the life. He never forgot them, but making time for them became more difficult.

#6 Recording 17:50 Miriam

Discussions, Questioning with Other Women

DS: When Miriam had her own life, she had good relationships with other women, and she raised questions with these women. Again, not trying to create doubt in faith but to explore faith. She had the mind, this is going to sound odd, but she had the mind of a man, the mind of a thinker. She would create discussions with other women around the well, around the laundry, about our faith, about our duty, about our God. She never weakened anyone's faith; she was careful with that. But she wanted people, the women, to think about what they did, what they believed, why they did it. **It was almost like she was trying to nurture something other than obedience, and she couldn't have even put it into words, but obedience wasn't enough.** It needed to be something else. *I have not a word to put to it, because she had not a word, but it had to be more than obedience.* There had to be more than obedience.

There were other women of like mind, not many, but there were interesting discussions about their faith, about their duty, about their role. When Miriam was in middle age, and she thought about it, she was quite different from her mother. It is like she copied her mother until she was twenty and then she started to stop copying her mother and actually be herself. She was herself, from the inside, different from her mother, but did not allow that to be witnessed or demonstrated until she was older, after twenty, we would say. Even then, she was careful, respectful, quietly obedient, but also quietly questioning. She was very good at not ruffling feathers. She did not ruffle feathers; she was not an irritant; she was not trying to stir the pot. **She was trying to understand so that her faith could be deeper.** She admired the faith of Moses. She didn't understand it and she wanted to understand it. It is interesting because it feels like she wanted to understand faith in order to have more faith. So, her faith was not a knowing of the heart, her faith was from an understanding.

As odd as it sounds, it feels like Miriam was educated. Her words are strong. She speaks well. Her voice is good. She knows how to say things, how to express herself, and she does it simply and succinctly. She does not use a lot of words, almost as if she knows she has someone's attention for a limited period of time so she must say this succinctly and quickly. She learns to do that. She learned to do that with Moses, because Moses tried to give her time when she was young and he was young, but he always had other things. So, she had to be quick about it when she had time with Moses. So that was sort of the training ground.

When she spoke succinctly and clearly with the women it gave them lots of time to think about the question she had asked, because she did not sermonize to them. She simply asked questions, and let them think about those questions. Then it might be weeks before they discussed those questions again. They might never discuss them, though often she wanted to. She didn't want to just ask open ended questions. She wanted to know what they, the women, felt; how they would answer. So, she would bring the questions up again weeks later. Miriam had a patience in her as she aged, a trust of life and self, and somehow that nurtured her patience. She was very observant.

#6 Recording 22:46 *Miriam*

Her Leadership in the Tribe

DR: She was a leader among the women of the tribe? Is that correct?

DS: We would not say that she was a leader, we would say this: She was a leader, but it would not have been acknowledged to her. The only leader she recognized was Moses. Miriam was an influence. If you would ask her to describe herself, she would say an influence. She asked questions, thought-provoking questions. She taught the young ones to think for themselves, to realize why things were done this way, not to simply try and remember how to do it. So, from our perspective in the now time, we might call her a leader, but she would not call herself such. She did recognize her influence and she took it seriously, but she would not let us call her a leader.

#6 Recording 23:43 *Miriam*

Her Impact on the Tribe and Beliefs

DR: How would you describe her impact on the tribe and the beliefs?

DS: Among the women she affected obedience the most. So rather than someone learning the steps to doing something, she helped them understand why the steps were this way, why you had to do things in this order of operation. So, there was a teacher within her that was trying to help those young ones understand what they were doing, why they were doing it this way in this order. So, it wasn't just a case of memory and obedience. She was influencing among the women, obedience. It does not feel like her influence was as such with the men. She was allowed the ear to question here and there, not often. There was some patience with certain men closer to Moses, because of who she was connected to Moses.

Her questions with Moses and one or two, three others, were almost always answered and they were questions of faith, questions about duty, questions about God. She had to be very careful she did not overstep. Miriam had been chastised by Moses once, maybe twice, and she learned her lesson young that there were certain questions about God she was not to ask, and so she was careful. Her influence with the men we would say, sometimes caused them to think more deeply or to consider something from a viewpoint they hadn't before. But they would never attribute this new viewpoint to the woman. It would be their own; they would make it their own.

#6 Recording 25:58 Miriam

Miriam and Aaron Dispute Moses

DR: There is a bible story about Miriam and Aaron, the other brother, challenging, going against Moses at one point. Can you explain this?

DS: This feels slightly exaggerated, but it is based in truth. It was the second time Miriam was chastised for her questions. She asked questions of God, of Moses in quiet, and was overheard by Aaron, and Moses chastised her. It was the chastisement that Aaron heard, not the question. Moses took her question to be questioning God itself, faith itself, and he was harsh with her. So, from those looking on they would see her challenging Moses, but she was not. She had asked a question. It was one of the times, we want to say, it was the last time she overstepped the mark with her questions and Aaron became involved when he heard Moses in anger.

Can we know the nature of the question, anything around the question, please? Show me now.

I cannot see the question clearly, but the sense I have is that it was around punishments, laws, duties, and their connection to God. "Why would God want that?" "Why would God need that?" Moses took this to be a question of faith. God did not need them to do anything: God wanted them to do it for their own good, to demonstrate their faith.

Always her problem was with obedience. Miriam was only questioning obedience, but it was seen as far deeper by Moses and it created chastisement. From the outside looking in, people would say that she had challenged him. If she did, it was not intended as such. It was just merely another question, the kind of questions she would only ask of Moses. But she overstepped the mark this time, went too far, and it feels like that created a little bit of an estrangement. Moses did not have as much time for her questions after that. He did not want to encourage her questioning God, questioning faith. He would let her question the ways, he would let her question the duties, but not the faith.

So, that did change things for her and she was treated with more wariness by the other men, for if Moses had gotten angry with her, they needed to be careful with her. It did not seem to affect her relationship with the women, but it definitely affected her relationship with the men. So, there is truth to the story, but from her perspective, she was not challenging Moses; she was wanting to understand God and it was not seen that way.

#6 Recording 29:45 Miriam

Relationship with Aaron

DR: So, Aaron went to her defence it would seem. What was her overall relationship with Aaron, who apparently was the brother of Moses and Miriam?

DS: As odd as it will sound, it feels to us as if there wasn't a deep relationship with Aaron. I will not say that this argument started the relationship with Aaron. It caused Aaron to see her differently, as if he had at times almost overlooked her, took her for granted. He knew of her, he spoke to her, he had time for her occasionally. He sometimes took her questions but was impatient with her questions. Aaron expected more obedience from her, but somehow when this altercation happened with Moses, it changed things. It changed his view of her, and we want to say he listened to her more. He was more careful with her. When he saw her aggravate Moses, it interested him, and he wanted to know more of what this was about, because it feels like he didn't hear it all; he only heard the chastisement. So, from then on, when Moses was a little more distant, Aaron was a little closer, but Miriam was so careful now with her questions she did not question of Aaron the way she would have questioned of Moses.

Chapter Eleven

DEBORAH

Deborah, wife of Lappidoth, was a prophetess. She led Israel at that time. She used to sit under the Palm of Deborah, between Ranmah and Bethel in the hill country of Ephraim, and the Israelites would come to her for decisions. (Judges 4:4-5)

#6 Recording 31:34 *Deborah*

DR: The story of Deborah, who was a judge and prophetess in the Bible...

DS: Can you give me more of her place in the tribe in the time?

DR: She was connected with Barak, a war leader, and there was a fight with some enemies, a battle.

DS: And her name again, please.

DR: Deborah.

DS: Great strength. We want to say she did not know her place and did not care that she did not keep her place. Deborah was vocal, sometimes demanding. Clear, spoke her mind, but again did not do it with disrespect. There was a cleverness about her strategy in her mind. She gained the respect of the men around her. She saw things differently and was very careful how she relayed information or questions to the men. She understood her place though she did not want to keep her place. She had opinions on things, ideas on things, that women were not supposed to have, and other women would not speak. She sometimes found her way to speak to them and she would be listened to, because there was a wisdom, a strategy in her approach. She was fair-minded, but she did not keep her place.

There was a man's strength; there was a man's reason within her. That is how she would have been seen by them, as if she had qualities that were not of a woman. Deborah was a puzzle, but there was also something special, *I don't know if that's the right word*, there was respect of the men towards her, almost as if they felt like God must have given her these wisdoms, these perspectives. And so, there was a special treatment to her sometimes. They could not imagine that a woman could think such or come to such reasoning on her own. And so, it was a gift from God, and because God gifted her with some of this, she was listened to in ways she might not have been in other situations.

There is a strength in her, like a female warrior strength, a strength of will. There was a passion in her, and she was quick to anger. She believed her beliefs strongly and did not bend. Compromise was difficult, and it was only that special status that allowed her to get away with this, not to be whipped, not to be punished.

In her childhood it was remembered that there were special moments, moments in prayer that would be almost meditative or trance-like. She never spoke any wisdoms, but other women noticed that she went deep somewhere in her prayers. And so, when the men, if the man complained about her as a woman, their wives would remember the child who could grow very quiet and very still and hold prayer space very well, as if she was connected to God. She was not saintly, and we will say that these memories often came to support the reasoning that it could not be her mind that came up with such strategy or such idea. It had to be a gift from God.

The story around Deborah was created to prove that she was no prophet, no saint; she was a clear thinker. Her mind was strong. She was observant and she put things together. She put pieces of puzzles together, people together. She could understand behaviour and motivation. She was very, very intelligent. It was almost unheard of for a woman to have such intelligence, and that is why it was reasoned to be a gift of God, a message of God itself. Deborah accepted this because it gave her freedom. She didn't fight the titles they gave her because it gave her the freedom to be who she needed to be, to speak as she needed to speak.

There were times where she would say that her ideas sometimes were God given. But there was pride in her and more often, she wanted the credit. But she understood that if God had the credit, she could speak more freely, and so she allowed it. But she would not think of herself as God directed or a prophet in any way. She just saw the world differently, observed things that went overlooked by others, particularly women. Again, it was like she had the mind of a man, the eyes of a man, the skills, the observation of a man. That's how it would have been described then, but it was not. It was her. It was the evolution of her.

#6 Recording 38:16 Deborah

Guiding Barak

DR: So, the story of Deborah and the war leader, Barak, her getting him to go to battle, this is a true story?

DS: Getting him to "go" to battle feels overstated. There was a strategy. She understood what he wanted to achieve, and she could see how the battle could achieve it. She made observations in the ears of the right people. It is not certain she had the ears of Barak, but she did contribute to the battle definitely. It feels overstated to say she initiated it; she didn't. She had opinions. She just saw things in the dynamics of relationship, in the hierarchy of power. She saw and understood what Barak wanted and saw ways and means to achieve it. As we have said, this was accepted almost as if it was God given to her for them.

#6 Recording 39:24 Deborah

Not a Prophetess or Medium

DR: So, Deborah was not really a prophet or even a medium who could receive messages?

DS: It does not feel so to us. It feels as if that was the story made, so that the men would not lose faith, wrong word, lose face in something she saw, that they did not; something she thought that they could not. So, the title was bestowed upon her, and she accepted it. It just feels to us that Deborah was a very clear thinker, highly observant, and strategic in her mind. Her faith was present, but it did not dominate her. Her relationship with God was important, but it did not dominate. So, we cannot call her prophetess.

#6 Recording 40:30 Deborah

A Leader in her Own Right

DR: So, in her own way, Deborah was a true leader of the tribe?

DS: And she would have loved to be called that but would never have used the words. She did see ways and means to achieve what they needed, what the tribe needed. There was inspiration to this one. We would say that there were miracles in that she was in the right place at the right time, happy coincidences to witness conversations between people, observe connections to people that others missed. So, there was some inspiration involved in her thinking, but it was Deborah who put the pieces together.

Chapter Twelve

RUTH AND NAOMI

But Ruth replied, "Do not urge me to leave you, to turn back and not follow you. For wherever you go I will go; Wherever you lodge, I will lodge; your people shall be my people, and your god, my god." (Ruth 1:16)

#7 Recording 4:00 With Bible

DR: Let's start with the biblical story of Ruth and Naomi as told in the biblical Book of Ruth. The questions are about the truth of the story and the meaning of the story, why it was written.

DS: Of the two named, Ruth feels stronger and more dominant, but she would hesitate to be called a leader. She has a wisdom and a practicality about her, and it is that practicality that led to the stories and the teachings. Ruth feels direct to us, clear in purpose and in faith. She understands what is required of her and feels that she understands what is required of her from God. With humans, she could be described as difficult or willful, but the sense we have is she is decisive and clear. She spends time, hours, maintaining clarity and connection. Her prayer space is sacred.

When we move our focus to Naomi, she feels younger, more vibrant, but less focused, more willful but less wise. There's a stubbornness in her determination and an immaturity in her womanhood. She portrays herself strong and mature, but she is younger than her years and immature, sometimes selfishly so.

There is a respect between Ruth and Naomi, but simultaneously there's a rebellious challenge; the way a daughter would challenge her mother if she comes into womanhood. Naomi feels challenging to Ruth. From Ruth's perspective, she wishes to be fair, clear, understanding, but it feels as if Naomi makes that difficult. They have different strengths in their belief of God. For Naomi, it is a service that is required by law. For Ruth, it is a service out of love.

The soul that inhabited Ruth had other lifetimes in service to gods and goddesses, and at that point in her soul journey was truly experiencing a spiritual development of faith, a love of deity. Ruth's lifetime was important in that love of God. With Naomi it is different. We cannot attach the word "love" to Naomi. There's service; there's reverence; there's obedience; but there is not love. It feels like that's a bit of a contention between the two of them. It feels as if Ruth is more determined to make things work with Naomi, to see Naomi as she is, to allow Naomi as she is, to forgive her. But there is not the same patience from Naomi to Ruth. There is contention there. This be how we see the relationship between the two of them.

Are there questions specific to give you more information?

DR: Yes, the question is: why is this relationship or story of Ruth and Naomi so important that it has its own book in the Bible? What is the message? What's the meaning of recording this story?

DS: There was a respect of Ruth among the males in her tribe. There were some that were even shamed by her dedication, her faith, her love. It was almost as if this book of Ruth was written to recognize what she had achieved, how deep her faith was.

In another time, in another space, she might have been called a saint, but she did not want sainthood. This one was just a woman serving her God. It feels like the book became written because there were those among the tribe that wanted Ruth to be a teaching for other women, a teaching for others lacking faith or lacking dedication. So, part of the writing of this book was to set example, to provide a recognition.

There's something else here. *(Spoken softly.)*

This phrase is used by Donna when she is speaking what she is seeing and then senses something else present at a deeper level. As if the information given is at a shallow level, and then she can perceive something else that needs to be said. Once she is connected to that, the words that follow are relayed.

When the writings about Ruth began, it feels, as if most unusually, she was aware or included in some way, most unusual. But she did not want this to be about her, but about faith, about service, about dedication. She would not allow herself to be recognized. She would not allow any grandeur from that. She participated in the writings of the Book of Ruth and was allowed to do so. She was critical to ensure that these wisdoms were the truth, to the best of her awareness and knowledge. It was very unusual. She did not write them, but she was allowed to read them, and her opinions were included, *not included*, taken into account. Changes she would ask for were made. She was involved in the writing though she did not write it.

It was labeled "The Book of Ruth" because it was a tribute, a recognition. Her involvement changed that so that it wasn't a tribute. It was a book of learning. It was a book of teaching. It became important to her that if her name was attached to it, it would represent the faith that she had, and it was important to those who wrote it, because they wanted others to see Ruth as something to aspire to be. There was a lot of teaching around this book and its creation, and a lot of cooperation between males and females. It was unusual for Ruth to be allowed to read what was written, to suggest amendments to what was written and to be listened to. We do not see her writing any of it though. Does this answer your question?

DR: Yes.

Chapter Thirteen

ESTHER

Esther was taken to King Ahasuerus in his royal palace, in the tenth month, which is the month of Tebeth, in the seventh year of his reign. The King loved Esther more than all the other women, and she won his grace and favour more than all the virgins. (Esther 2:16-17)

#6 Recording 41:53 Esther

Story of Esther

DR: I wish to ask about the story of Esther, of the Book of Esther, who was in Persia and who saved her people.

DS: It is interesting as we connect to Esther, there's almost two people within her, the one she was in her youth and very different one in her womanhood. I can't see how she changed or what changed her though, but the Esther you ask of is not the Esther who was born. She was quiet, obedient, curious, and clever, but not one you would ever call a leader. Then something changed.

Can we see the events, please? Show me now.

It feels like something happened to her as if a violence was done to her, or she was involved in something. It erased her innocence, her naivety, and her self-defence ignited. It does not feel like a rape or violence that way. It feels more like she witnessed something that was cruel and unnecessary. The child mind, *I'm going to use the word "snapped"*, the child mind snapped, could not comprehend such irrational behaviour, such cruelty. Somehow within her something shifted, opened. A decision was made on an unconscious level, and she stepped out into a different place of herself, more defiant, more strong, more vocal, less obedient, less quiet, no longer easily intimidated. Those around her who would say she became difficult; some would even call it unreasonable. What she became was powerful and it is from here that the one you asked of was born.

Inside her heart she had the softness of her childhood, the innocence of her childhood, the understanding, compassion of her childhood. But she did not demonstrate that externally in the role you see her as. That role called her into another level of herself, another type of behaviour, and she was certain it was needed. Whatever she witnessed showed her that things had to change for her tribe, for her people. This type of behaviour could no longer be tolerated. Things had to change, and she decided to be part of that change. When she spoke of this to her mother, her mother was overwhelmed that her daughter would think such things and how could it possibly be for her. Yet it was. I'm not sure whose daughter she was. I'm not sure if she was in line for this leadership role, but what we're seeing is the internal birth of it. Her voice was strong, and she insisted on being heard, and she challenged things that she felt would nurture unreasonable behaviour.

#6 Recording 46:10 Esther

Married the King, Saved Her People

DR: The story that she married the king, I guess King Xerxes, and that she helped save the Hebrews?

DS: She married because there was power recognized in her. She was not disrespectful, but she did not hide herself; and she asked questions of the king. She asked questions of the people with the king. And it created curiosity and brought her to the king, because she was such a thinker, and she was such an observer. The king saw a way he could use her because she observed interactions. She observed looks and glances. She understood, *we're going to call it "politics", but it's not what it would have would have been called then.* She understood the politics, and the king saw an advantage to her. And the king did not marry her out of love or lust, but he saw she could be useful to him, and she proved to be so. He gave her license to ask questions. He spent time alone with her, and as his wife, he was allowed to do so. So, she influenced him; she helped him to see through things, and she helped to undo scandals and undo, undo things that shouldn't come to pass. He was known to be powerful without anyone understanding that she was the power behind the throne.

He very much came to love her, but it cannot be said that he didn't love her for the power it gave him. I don't know if he loved her for the woman she was, but he loved his relationship with her. He loved how they were, what they discussed, what she saw, what they questioned. She very much was the power behind the throne. Not that he could not be powerful without her, but he was more powerful with her.

#6 Recording 48:17 Esther

Haman and Esther

DR: The story of the evil man named Haman who wanted to wipe out the Hebrews and her role in that story?

DS: Intolerable behaviour could not be tolerated. Whatever she witnessed, this idea of Haman's, it was too close to what she had witnessed. She could see it could be done, and it could not be allowed. It was heinous to her; it was more than a sin. And so, her voice was loud around this, and she saw things in the eyes of Haman. She saw things in this man that others did not see, as if she could see into his heart, through his eyes. She could see his hatred. She could see his violence. She could see that if this was allowed it would lead to others, and she convinced her husband that if he did not stop this, he would be stopping many other things as if this was step one of five, not only one thing. She saw something that said that if this man is allowed to do this, he would do worse. And by that point the king listened to her. He valued her, and he knew she had insight into people. She could see inside people. She could see the evil in this one. It is why the word was used in the story, because she would have used the word herself, because it was so heinous what he wanted to do. There was so much hatred in him in the doing of it; there was no reason in it.

#6 Recording 50:02 *Esther*

Haman's Plan

DR: What was Haman attempting to do at first? What was he trying to do that she saw and put a stop to? What was the first thing he was trying to do that she objected to?

DS: Judging some as unfit. *I'm going to use these words, but they're not the right words,* pure blood, not pure enough, not holy enough, not of the tribe enough. There was some that weren't good enough, and they should not be allowed, weeded out. But Esther could see in his reasoned argument that this was not reason at all; that there was a hatred in him. We'll use the analogy, if he was allowed to take the weak ones from the tribe, he would then start to challenge the strong ones as well. Haman had other plans, she felt, other plans unspoken in his reasoning. Esther could see with him a lust for power and a hatred, deep judgment, a rigidity. And so, if he was allowed to cull the weak ones from the tribe, that it would not stop there. She could feel that. He had another agenda. She tried to make sense of what she saw, but the king merely feared that he would be challenged as king, and so took her at her word.

#6 Recording 52:07 *Esther*

Haman Wanted to Banish Unfit

DR: So, he actually wanted to kill the people he judged as unfit?

DS: At first it was more banishment, but that led to death, that would lead to death; and then because that would lead to death, it would then be more merciful to kill them. For them, without a tribe, they would die anyway, and that would be cruel. So, you see the reasoning was sound, but it was not sound to her. There was hatred in it. Haman did not speak of murder first. He spoke of it as banishment, and then to put them to death would be merciful.

#6 Recording 52:56 Esther

Plan Started Against the Hebrews

DR: He was Persian and not of the Hebrew tribe, correct?

DS: *I want to say that question doesn't matter. It doesn't feel like it was just about the Hebrews.* He was Persian, but it wasn't an attack against the Hebrews. *It was something else that started it.* There it is. It started with the Hebrews and that's what Esther saw. Esther saw that it would start with the Hebrews, and it would go further. Yes, he was Persian, but his plan only started with the Hebrews.

Above in this paragraph, the words in italics show you the process that Donna goes through to be clear in what it is, exactly, that Esther understood. Here there is a slight departing from the story, in that it was not just, or only, about the Hebrews. As Donna perceives Esther and her understandings, it takes her into an understanding of Haman. It takes Donna into the same understanding of Haman that Esther had. Fascinating.

#6 Recording 54:17 Esther

Haman Had Power in Court

DR: Was Haman high in the Persian court? Had he power in the court with the king?

DS: Haman had power generationally. He was not popular in court, but he had a place in court because of his generational line. There was a concern if he grew too popular in the court, *I can't see what that's about*, but he wasn't popular in the court. He had a place in court, yes. He had power in court, yes, because it couldn't be taken from him, not really. So, he had to be curtailed another way. He had to be controlled.

Chapter Fourteen

SAMPSON AND DELILAH

After that, he fell in love with a woman in the Wadi Sorek, named Delilah. The Lords of the Philistines went up to her and said, "Coax him and find out what makes him so strong, and how we can overpower him, tie him up, and make him helpless, and we'll give you eleven hundred shekels of silver." (Judges 16:4-5)

#7 Recording 14:06 *Sampson and Delilah*

Story of Sampson and Delilah

DR: Switching to another story, the famous story of Sampson and Delilah.

DS: There are several purposes to this story. It is loosely based on real people. It was written as a story of warning. It was written more like a parable. But when it was written it was also a chastisement, a small amount of ridicule for the people it was loosely based on. This is a story about selfishness; the story about putting the self ahead of others.

It created a stir among the women when it was written, for the character of Delilah was based on a selfish woman. There was upset among the women that they were unfairly represented, and it did result in some *what word can we use…*the woman that it was loosely based on was not ostracized or rejected, but she was sort of given the cold shoulder by the other women. They could not exclude her, but where they could ignore her, they did. It was felt to be unfair to the women that all were judged by her, that the story was exaggerated and unfair.

The men took the story more seriously, and felt chastised, and saw a …teaching? *(There is hesitation in the audio as Donna understands what this story was to the men.)* A teaching, a warning within it; a warning about the way of the flesh, a warning about the women, which is again another upset to the women themselves. It feels as if it was written by one cleric, one rabbi? I'm not sure. *Again, Donna hesitates as she understands what she is seeing.* But it was written by one who was… *vindictive is too strong of a word.* This one who wrote this story was black and white – strict, unforgiving. He was focused on the sins of men. This one wrote other stories about the sins of men and wanted to eradicate sin. He was harshly strict and judgmental, did not, interestingly, did not practice forgiveness within himself, as if forgiveness only came from God. And so, there was an odd lack of forgiveness about this man. Feels as if he wrote two or three other stories, harsh stories, harsh results, and could not be persuaded to soften his tone or change his writings in any way. He was dedicated to what he was doing, believed in it in a black and white way. It feels as if this story was a bone of contention. It created upset in the women; it created a harshness in the men. It brought question to forgiveness. There were those who wrote the stories, who worked on the text of the Bible, who were not certain it should be included. It did, even within the masters of the tribe, create discussion and disagreement. But the merit of its teachings is how it was decided to be included to the Bible. So, there is a lot of contention, argument, and discussion in the history of this story.

#7 Recording 20:12 Sampson and Delilah

Who was Delilah?

DR: Was Delilah a Hebrew woman or a Philistine as in the story?

DS: She was based upon a Hebrew woman made Philistine to make the story more palatable. It was one of the changes that the writers agreed upon. But it was mostly based upon a Hebrew woman. It doesn't feel like there was a Delilah. It feels like it was a representation in the writer's mind of the sin of woman, of the evil of woman.

#7 Recording 21:02 Sampson and Delilah

Sampson's Powers

DR: The Sampson it was based upon, did he have great strength?

DS: Not in literal sense of body. It was a generalization that demonstrated the strength of men that wanted men to find their strength, to be that strength. So, it was not literally physical strength.

#7 Recording 21:32 Sampson and Delilah

Selfishness

DR: Was he the selfish one?

DS: The sense we have is that there was selfishness and wanton recognized in both of them and wanted to be recognized in both of them. There were selfish goals, thoughtless actions, careless behaviour, and so it feels to us as if both were, so to speak, in the wrong.

#7 Recording 22:03 Sampson and Delilah

Sampson's Physical Strength

DR: Then the story of Sampson having great physical strength and the strength was in his hair. When Delilah cut his hair, he lost his strength. This is all fabricated?

DS: It feels like a parable. The one who wrote it had a warning to men of male vanity, of male wantonness, of body desire, of body admiration. It was the shallowness of it all. *There's something else here… Creator why the hair to the strength, show me that now, please.*

It feels symbolic. It feels as if the strength of men is not to be connected to his external features or his vanity, but to his faith. When it's put elsewhere, when it's valued differently, then the strength becomes weakness. What is interesting to us, as we perceive this, is we can sense the message the writer wanted to pursue, to say in the story, but it doesn't feel like what this one was trying to write about was clear in his story. It was clear in his mind. But in the symbolism it was not clear, and so it almost requires us to explain it, because it isn't obvious. It was obvious in his mind. But his mind was quite narrow and quite angry, almost hateful at times. It feels to us as if there were problems with this one *(the writer of the story)* with women, with relationships, with his strength as a man, his strength with his brothers. And so, the symbolism within the story is not as obvious to the reader as it was to the writer.

In the above paragraphs, there are several places where Donna is hesitating in how to express what she is perceiving. This happens from time to time, because the selection of the words used to express the information is very important. Sometimes Donna "tries" a word to see if it fits. In the trying, she realizes it is too strong of a word, and must pause to find the correct word that relays the truth of the moment she is perceiving.

As well, when we are describing the man who wrote this story, our connection to him is complete. We are perceiving his personality and his faith. Within him there is almost an angry vehemence against sin, and that very much colors what and how he writes. We can feel his dedication to his writing and his need to "wipe out" sin. And then we see him and his approach with all he writes, and the contention it created with the other writers of the Bible themselves. It is fascinating to perceive. As we continued to explore the writer of this story, we were able to perceive his personality, his relationship to his life and found that his faith was very important to him, but that his approach adversely affected all the relationships within his life. Truly, he was a dedicated man, but within that dedication to God, he expected such perfection that he had unreasonable expectations of people. Fascinating.

Chapter Fifteen

DIVINE BEINGS TAKING DAUGHTERS OF MEN

The divine beings saw how beautiful the daughters of men were and took wives among them that pleased them. (Genesis 62)

#7 Recording 34:37 *Biblical Line – Divine Beings*

Divine Beings Taking Daughters of Men

DR: There is a Bible passage about divine beings taking daughters of men for wives. Can you explain that statement?

DS: This came from a dream... a vision of the writer. It was dreamed so often he was uncertain whether it was a dream, a vision, or a reality. And yet, there was never anyone missing from the tribe to prove it a reality.

There was great discussion of this vision, and it was only brought into discussion because it was dreamed by the dreamer several times, four or five times, the same dream. So, it was brought to the circle as a question for discussion. It's hard for us to discern its meaning because there were theories and discussions and symbolisms discussed, wonderings. In actuality there was never any missing women in a physical way. There were at times, thought among the men, among the circle of discussion, that some women changed greatly, quickly, and there was a wondering if something in the dream had caused the women to change, mature, grow, in the way they did so quickly, as if there was a visitation. In the circle of men that discussed it, more of them believed this was about a visitation to the women, than of a taking of them.

But, the line was never changed, because the one who had the vision would not allow it. He did not see it as a visitation. He saw a taking, and so the line was written as it was. But, for most of those who agreed to the inclusion of the line in the writing, they felt it was more representative of a visitation, and that was supported by some of the growth and wisdom that some women seemed to acquire quickly. It was as if there was a maturing within them, that did not take years or even months, sometimes only weeks.

They decided among themselves that this vision was to let them know this was divine and that this visitation as they chose to see it was of God, was from God, and was for the betterment of the women. But there was disagreement among the one who had the vision. This one never really believed it was a visitation, and was alert and watching for changes in women, for any women that came or went from the tribe. But there was very little evidence in the physical reality to support his vision, and so it does feel like it became nothing more than a line. There never was another story about it or more writings connected to it.

#7 Recording 38:58 Biblical Line - Divine Beings

Who Wrote the Line?

DR: Who was the dreamer who wrote this line? When did it occur, earlier in the story of the Hebrews or much later?

DS: Much later. The writings of the Bible were two-thirds completed. This one wanted the entire vision in the story, *wrong word*, written as a story for the writings of the Bible, but it was after much discussion reduced to the one line. There was not enough to merit it as a parable or story.

#7 Recording 40:18 Biblical Line-Divine Beings

Incomplete Story

DR: So, what was left out?

DS: The entire details of the dream and vision. This line

represented the vision, but did not detail the vision. There was, in a vision, a removal of the women, one or two at certain seasons of the year, and then they were returned before the next season. They were gone days or a week or two, and they always came back changed – stronger, clearer, voice stronger, mind stronger, will stronger. It was the entire vision that was left out. It was boiled down to just the one line.

#7 Recording 41:24 Biblical Line – Divine Beings

Role of Dreamer

DR: Did this dreamer have a position of influence in the tribe?

DS: It feels as if he was connected to one of the writers, one of the storytellers, brother, cousin. It was through that connection he was connected to the writer.

Chapter Sixteen

SUMMARY: MALE-FEMALE POWER BALANCE

Note: The following summary includes both recordings and post-recording discussions with the latter noted.

#6 Recording 1:04:50 *Women Influenced by Asking Questions*

DS: So interesting as we finish that, that most of the influence those women had was more by asking questions. I find that interesting. It's like they weren't allowed to know or say, but they were allowed to question. As if the questions, there was a feeling as if when they ask questions, it was this, this weakness trying to understand. It appealed to the men to answer the questions, because the man knew and the women didn't know. It didn't feel like the women told anybody anything. It felt more like they questioned. I find that interesting and that seems common.

DR: That is happening from the very beginning. So, when we talked about the Matriarchs, the very first session, that they, instead of telling them that (for example) "Oh, you should do this," they asked questions, to prompt them (the men) in the right direction. That story in the Matriarchs, and especially the story of Rachel, who met with Jacob, in which she dared to question him.

DS: That's interesting, I didn't remember that.

DR: That's the theme all throughout here, is the way to prod and get them (the men) to think.

DS: Then when she asked the questions, when we were talking about Miriam and Moses, that argument with Moses, she went too far with her question. She questioned something that Moses did faithfully, it was faith in God; you didn't question that. I couldn't see what it was, but it was like, "Well, you don't question that," you know.

DR: The stories were excellent. They really filled out the personalities and the growth in these women from a youngster to adulthood, and then to more mature adults. But that's something you don't get in the Bible stories, the actual growth of human beings and how they will change. These women are mentioned in the Bible, but the strength of them, like Esther. So, Esther and Deborah, were very, very strong women who spoke their minds for the most part, it's quite fascinating.

DS: If I would label Deborah by what I know now, I would call her a Matriarch, and Matriarch for me means they took no bullshit, like clear, concise, speak the truth, no fancy words, just do it. It was interesting, because she allowed them to attribute her, her intelligence to God, but she didn't believe it. She was inspired, but she was just a clear thinker. She observed people and could put two and two together in a way that others didn't. It was a strategy in her mind. She did have a very strong male energy; she had a very strong mind. She found a way not to get it subjugated. It's interesting, what we've talked about today, that's how I see people (in channel). Like that's my only way to read a person, is to go inside out and see where their starting points are and how they evolve, and how they become. I don't read them from the outside in. I read them from the inside out. It's interesting.

DR: What we see throughout the stories is that the men had trouble accepting women as their equals, in equality, in speaking out, in power. So, like in the case of Deborah, so they ascribe her getting divine inspiration so that they can accept, okay, she has something valid to say. That to me is another huge thing throughout that is coming about through the stories.

DS: It feels to me that there was a pride in the men that couldn't allow a woman to see something they missed or be smarter than them. So, things had to be attributed to God, because it couldn't have been in the woman. Truly, we have seen it consistently, that they have a place. I seem to remember when we talked about Sarah, that Sarah was teaching women to be more than that.

We did, if I remember it correctly, say that Sarah was teaching them how to be a better wife to their husband. So even in that, the husband would get, shall we call it, the glory or the credit for what the wife would bring to the husband's awareness. So, it is interesting, I wonder why. I wonder where...

DR: But even that teaching of Sarah, for the women to have a mind of their own got squashed quite quickly after that.

DS: I don't remember that, but I would be curious to know, when in the history the women became subjugated, what caused that. Were they ever equal, you know? Like my feeling for Eden is that Eve was equal to Adam and never felt like Eve was subjugated.

DR: Yes, my recollection is that Eve and Adam were basically on equal par, and Sarah and Abraham were almost (at) equality. But soon after that, and there was an incident where the men just took over. It was the story of Dinah in the Bible. It said that a guy from outside the tribe had raped her and then he wanted to marry her, and then the whole retaliation happened. It wasn't that at all. She had started talking to a guy who was helping teach her and learn.

DS: Yes, I remember now. It would be interesting if we could track when the equality of Eve, how it devolved. What was the difference between the time of Eve and the time of Sarah, and then how did it devolve even further so that women could question but not speak. I would love to know that because I didn't feel that in Eden. I didn't see it or feel it in Eden. It was there in Sarah and it was trying to come back in Sarah. How did it even (happen) if it only devolved one step, how did that happen? I just wondered if (it had) anything to do with leaving Eden, you know. Then the strength of the men kept the family alive when they were hunting and hoarding and protecting. I don't know. It would be an interesting question about how the role of women devolved, where did it devolve, where did women lose their equality and how or why, if it can be articulated.

DR: I think it was continual downgrading and some women tried to bring it back up. But it was a continual fight for millennia. We see it today, seriously, the women's movement of the 60s and the Me Too (movement). We see the fight continuing today. It is ridiculous.

DS: In metaphysics, I was taught by some teacher, I don't remember who, that there was a point on the earth where the Goddess decided to step back, so the ego God could step forward. The ego was going to be developed on the earth for a while and so Goddess stepped back to allow that ego to develop, that male aspect to develop. That it was a choice, that there was an equality between God and Goddess and then Goddess stepped back and God developed, and now Goddess is coming back. There are those among my profession who think Goddess must now step forward. I am not one of them. I think now Goddess wants to return to equality, not to dominance. It is almost like Goddess did not get her chance to dominate, so it's "wait a minute, it's my turn now", among some of the women that I work with. I don't get that. I don't know where that came from. I must ask David if he knows where he got that. Metaphysically that's something that's discussed energetically on the planet to explain the dominance of male energy on the planet in the subjugation. But I'd like to know that from Eden; that would be fascinating; that would be fascinating.

#7 Recording 58:12 Evolutionary Impact on Male–Female

Evolutionary Effect More than Energy Effect

DS: There were so many strands connected to evolution that I couldn't generalize them, but what was interesting was that even though we approached it as a suppression of women, I could feel that it was an evolutionary effect. The balance on earth rather than the energy, the balance on earth was changing and growing and evolving, and then that balance of earth demonstrated through the male-female relationships, obviously so, in the tribes with their laws, but also not so obviously in other tribes in other ways, quite interesting to feel that evolutionary effect on the relationships in the male and female development and relationship. The very essence of it quite interesting.

DR: So, the evolutionary change kind of pushed the male to try to take more power or deny power?

DS: No, what it was as I perceived; it was that the evolution was increasing the female and then there was a male response to that increase. Then that itself became... everything we do here becomes evolved so the females were evolving; they created a reaction in the males; the males reacted and then as the males reacted, how they reacted and how they controlled, how they suppressed, also evolved. That's why it's so complicated to even try and put it into words, because every choice and decision is then affected, is then taken into the evolution of the character the evolution, of the choice. It feels more like it was evolution that caused the women to grow stronger, and then the males reacted to that and then evolution acted the other way.

Very interesting, confusing almost. I do remember a teacher at some point in the last 30 years saying that there was a point on the planet where in order to have an experience of ego, the female energies decided to allow themselves to be suppressed so the male energies could increase, and the school of earth could have the experience of ego directed by male, directed by pride, directed by intellect. The teacher who said that, I don't remember who it was, said that that's where we got into the years of industrial revolution and all the innovation because intellect was running the world, so to speak. Then now, I don't know remember when because this was so long ago, but my perception is that in the eighties and nineties, probably a harmonic convergence in 1988, the female energy said, "Okay enough; now let's restore balance." Now, we've been working, probably even before that, because we had women's lib, and I don't remember when, but I know that in the harmonic convergence there was a distinct change with the earth in her relationship to male and female. At some point then, the female energies started to grow again and not be dominated, refused the domination as if that chapter of us allowing this is now over, and let's go back to balance. I believe that, this is just a personal belief, that what's going on in our world now is a restoration of balance between male-female intellect, emotion, all of that. There's a balance that can be achieved here, an equal partnership that I don't think we've experienced on the earth for millennia. I believe there was female dominant, then male dominant, and the error, in my opinion, would be to go back to female dominant. We need to go back to balance. And it's like we're trying to find balance and we can't find it. We go from one dominance to another dominance, when really, we're supposed to have balance, but that's just my own opinion from what I've seen and experienced.

DR: So, when you have visions of what was happening, now do you see the direction of the present onwards? Do you see it still bouncing around or moving in a favourable direction?

DS: I didn't look forward. What I looked for was to see how evolution, like I sort of went through this view of evolution's influence, and so I saw the ebbs and flows, not even all the way to the present moment. I was trying to see how evolution affected those choices when women were suppressed in the tribes. I didn't see it clearly. I just had this sense of so much more going on than what we were talking about; that it was just one event in a whole scenario that was unfolding.

#7 Recording 1:03:37 Evolutionary Impact on Male-Female

Stories Written as Parables; Moral Messages

DR: Very interesting that the story of Sampson and Delilah, the story of the divine being taking women, were stories with little or no truth behind them. They were written for parables, moral messages.

DS: Yes, that's what I would call them. Presented as a real story, but really a parable. There were discussions; this wasn't done easily. There were discussions, grand discussions for weeks to decide what they would include, what they wouldn't include, how the tone of it would be. I don't think it was complete agreement; yet, at that stage of writing of the suppression of women, I think there was movement towards it. It felt more like women started to be perceived as a threat, and had a manmade error in judgment. They wouldn't have been as punished as the women. It was like they took a risk, listening to a woman, and then when it didn't work out it was like, "See we shouldn't be doing this; we shouldn't be doing this". A lot of it always it feels to me, perfectly willing to be wrong, but it felt like a lot of it always came back to we must do God's will. This can't be God's will. We must do God's will. That's interesting, but it is also fascinating to me that… let's say, there was a circle of ten or twelve men that were influencing or running the tribe, writing the writings, how much influence they had. This wasn't a democracy. How much interest, how much influence they had by what was decided in that circle. See, the women had more influence in that circle at the time of Sarah, much more influence and in a very positive way, and then I could see the erosion. The questions raised in the third generation after Sarah, and then erosion really taking place in the fourth and fifth, and then suppression in the sixth. So, it did take a few generations for it to happen, but it was steadily incremental until it was finally at that point where "this is your place," you know.

#7 Recording 41:50 Women Kept from Power

DR: It seems from Eden all the way forward that women were kept in inferior positions power-wise, losing power. What was the reason for this and was there a turning point?

DS: I can see the movement of the women in their roles and, at first, we would object to your words. There was equality with the women and the man for a long time, and then there was a time where in several instances with men of particular power in the tribe, the women stood their ground and demanded certain changes, demanded to be heard. Up until then, the women exerted their influence through their husbands, and with other women through the teaching of the children. There was a time where, it's not that they wanted more, but they seemed stronger, their voices seemed louder, not literally, and there were some men who felt that this was going too far. There was the equality that was evolving, was too much, the women had too much power, and so then things started to be written and taught and women of softer voice, women of more agreeableness were valued more than those of strong will. There was a changing, and then, as this happened there were other men who wanted the less equality. They thought the equality was the problem; the equality was not of God's way; the equality was wrong in some way. It feels like there were several instances where a woman's opinion was followed and created more of a problem not less, was to be a solution that became a bigger problem. Then there was overreaction to those situations, and then the role of the women, they wrote it, the definition of a good wife changed. The definition of a good wife that would receive recognition and praise changed. The role of women, how do I explain this, it feels like writing said that God redefined, that God's role of women was not what women had become, and so then God's word was used to reduce their power in their place. It feels as if we would generalize that the equality the women were in started to threaten men, certain of the leaders, certain of the writers, and then it took, I want to say almost two generations before the women really lost their place. It was eroded with a steadiness and it feels like there was… if there were ten men of influence there was three or four, that, for lack of a better term, turned against the equality of women and then their influence spread. It took about two generations, and then the strengthening, the wisdom of Sarah and others like her was no longer respected, no longer encouraged, no longer rewarded. In fact, it was sometimes punished. It was a gradual thing. It wasn't overnight.

#7 Recording 46:37 *Women Kept from Power*

When Did Women Lose Power?

DR: About when did this happen especially the change in the

writings (which) said this is God's will or however they phrased it… about when did this happen?

DS: If we move from Sarah, *show me from Sarah please, Creator.* Sarah lived a long time, so it feels like she saw the beginnings of it at the time of her great-grandchildren, so not her children, not her grandchildren but her great-grandchildren. That was the generation that it started (in). Some of the counsels, some of the solutions provided by women seem to create some bigger problems. It then took two generations, it feels like, before it was really an issue, before it really started to suppress. At first it was more like an erosion, and then it changed attitude, law, and it really started to suppress.

Understood?

DR: Yes.

So, five, six generations from Sarah is when it really took hold?

DS: Yes, so generation 4 and 5 from Sarah is when the erosion was happening. Started in three (*note – generation 3 is of Dinah*) and eroded in four and five, and in five and six it was suppression.

Understood?

DR: Yes.

#7 *Recording 48:37 Issue Today with Power of Women*

Reason for Continued Power Issue Today

DR: So why today is this still being a fight over male versus female power and suppression of women thousands of years later? Why is it still a fight?

DS: The fight that is in your world now is beyond the religions, beyond the tribes. It's hard to generalize this. It is an energetic shift from intellect to heart to feeling. It is a partnership in building between the equality of intellect and emotion between male and female energy. It feels like there was, even in the God itself, there was more male than female, and then over the last thousand years the female essence of God has been getting stronger.

There's something around mother Earth and father God. There are several different energies that feed into this. *Can you show me this, mother Earth - father God as it relates to the time of the women's suppression that we were just talking about?* It is something in evolution that started in the tribes we were just discussing, the five generations from Sarah. There's something evolutionary about it, was something about re-balancing on the planet in an evolutionary way. There was so much innovation and invention and mind driven directions, intellect, learning. Then the arts also evolved, but they were not as important. It feels evolutionary and it feels like the evolution actually did affect what occurred in the tribe, what began in the tribe in the third, fourth generation from Sarah. It didn't just come from males. It came from the evolution, the evolutionary energy that was an evolution of strength; and then there was an evolution of loss of strength with females, and then an evolution of strength again.

So, we can see the evolution playing a part in this, but it's very hard to generalize it, because it has streams where evolution had focus in like five or six different places, different demonstrations of this male-female evolution. We can't call it conflict. It's the evolution of the male-female gender, the male-female energies, the male-female creation, the male-female power, the male-female demonstrations. So, it's part of the evolution, that evolutionary energy on the planet affected, not just gender relationships, but the actual energies of male and female, yin and yang.

CONCLUSION

This story of *Women of the Hebrew Bible* is not finished. It is just the beginning. In simply asking questions, we received information that is awe-inspiring, that paints a whole different picture of these women whose lives were recorded in the Hebrew Bible. Whether one believes that these stories are just fiction or contain truth or are somewhere in between, they are certainly fascinating and should give most people pause for reflection.

In this Q&A channelled format, I (Dan) had prepared questions which were not disclosed in advance to Donna. In addition, many questions arose in real time as the answers were received. In some cases, we pursued a new unexpected topic before returning to the main line of questions. It became readily apparent that there was far more information and directions that could be pursued about each person or event. We tried to keep each one-hour session for each person of interest, but could have continued for ten hours, and still not gotten all the questions answered. That is why I say that this is just the beginning, not the finish of this work.

The story that emerged from the questions was equality between male and female at the beginning and subsequent erosion of that equality over generations. As seen in some of the texts in the *Summary: Male - Female Power Balance* section, that imbalance is a little complex, not just of males trying to dominate. It may have involved alternating changes in male/female power over long periods of time, as well as impacts due to evolution. In another book we are working on, it was noted that evolution on Earth is a very strong continuing force and affects all activities including ideas, technology, thinking patterns, biology, and more. In clarifying how this imbalance came to be, in understanding its origins, we can decide to restore balance – for the good of humanity.

BIBLIOGRAPHY

Biblical quotes

The Torah: The Five Books of Moses.1962. Jewish Publication Society of America. Philadelphia.

Tanakh: The Holy Scriptures: 1985. Jewish Publication Society. Philadelphia.

ACKNOWLEDGEMENTS

From Dan Ronis

This book is dedicated to my mother Geraldine Ronis (nee Zendel) a teacher, a feminist, a shy spiritual woman who loved learning above all else and who encouraged me from above.

I am grateful for the four women who helped birth this book: Donna Somerville, my co-author, who generously donated her time and talent, to Patricia Dale who for her insight and guiding words, to my editor, Fay Thompson, who artfully crafted the book into its final form with a woman's touch, and to Kelsey Pavier who whose artwork graces the cover.

To the women who unknowingly helped inspire this book by living lives of strength, integrity, and faith, Esther Turner (Washington D.C.) and sisters Beryl and Karen Stovell (Ontario, Canada).

Lastly, my life has been greatly enriched these last almost fourteen years thanks to my wife and partner, Nancy A. Lease.

From Donna Somerville

When I considered acknowledgements for my part in this book, they are first to those people who demonstrated what could be accessed through "channeling" and how they generously taught and encouraged me in that direction. Of course, next is my husband, David Somerville, who has stood by me and supported me since 1988, through an interesting and varied journey of life. We met in a meditation class and began exploring from that point until now. Our journey of discovery continues.

Specifically, I want to name those that demonstrated what channeling could be. First, now passed away, Barbara Eagles (Ontario, Canada) who scared me with what she could access and bring through. And then, Frank Alper (Arizona, USA), also passed away, who demonstrated the next level of channel. And then finally, multiple teachers who generously encouraged me in a direction I explored with trepidation and uncertainty of which my most influential was Bonnie Bielous (Minnesota, USA). Thank you to them all.

Thank you to the many clients, who over these years, have trusted me to open and see for them, thereby stretching me in new directions. My practice with them has led me to what I was able to bring through for this book.

To Dan, who asked, "could you answer some questions" and trusted me to do so. Thank you.

And finally, to my inner self who has so bravely travelled "the road less travelled" and done so with grace and wonderful faith. And, of course, to the souls of these interesting women of the Hebrew Bible, who have opened themselves to me, so that we could explore and understand the lives they lived and how they lived them. Thank you.

ABOUT THE AUTHORS

DANIEL H. RONIS is a retired scientist whose lifelong interest in religions and spiritual knowledge has led to the creation of this book. He is continuing this lifelong adventure taking courses in religious studies at a local university as part of a certificate in Jewish-Christian origins. He is hopeful that this effort will continue with one or more additional books on topics of personal interest.

DONNA SOMERVILLE is not an author, but a channel. One who has learned and then practised the art of opening to another place in space and time, to bring through wisdoms and perspectives to help change how we view the lives we live and how we live them. Donna has been doing this channeling work full time since 1994. The use of channel in creating this book took her work in a new direction. Donna had worked with other authors, but in a very arms length approach. These channelings with Dan are much more involved and much more intriguing; a real step away from the one on one, personal channelings Donna has been doing for so long.

www.ingramcontent.com/pod-product-compliance
Lightning Source LLC
Chambersburg PA
CBHW071322120626
46546CB00002B/406